Dear America

A Breakup Letter

Benjamin Gorman

To the Country I Believed In

And All Those I Love

And Am Leaving Behind

Dear America

A Breakup Letter

Dear America,

I won't sugarcoat this: Breakups are hard. But sometimes they are the best option.

This will not be the most difficult breakup I've survived, and it will be painless for you. You have a lot bigger problems to deal with than one small-town English teacher hopping on a plane and getting the heck out of Dodge.

Before I go further, I want to make something clear: I am not saying everyone should break up with you, America. Some people have been uncomfortable around me since they've heard we're breaking up, and I've come to learn they are worried I'll scold them for not doing what I'm doing. Others are uncomfortable because they want to break up with you, also, and can't for a host of reasons. I totally respect them and am not trying to persuade anyone to do what I'm doing. My circumstances are unique, or at least unusual. More on that later.

Believe it or not, this isn't even the first time I've broken up with someone in written form. To my great embarrassment, I confess I once broke up with a serious girlfriend via email. In my defense, I thought we had wrapped up the painful in-person discussion and mutually agreed to continue it via email, so I went home and crafted my thoughts in the format I (selfishly) prefer. After the break up, she told people I dumped her via email, which is technically correct but makes me look worse without the context, and I suppose I deserve that. I figure, if it hurt her, then I was at fault. I'll just go on feeling guilty about that long after she's forgotten about me or has relegated me to an anecdote about an unfortunate thing that happened to her one time. That's how I roll. And I expect you'll end up feeling much the same, America. I was just someone who was here for 47 years, mostly made a positive impact by teaching four or five thousand of your kids, wrote some books nobody read and published some books by other authors people should read more, and then disappeared from your life.

But I want to offer you something of value before I go, America, because I still love you. Please, even if you don't care at all about me, consider my advice. Breakups are an opportunity to reflect, to sit in our newly empty spaces and see ourselves as we truly are. If we're brave enough, they can be the motivation to do the hard work of opening ourselves up for change.

America, you need some serious therapy.

Who Is Dumping Whom?

In some breakups, it's very clear who is dumping whom. I've been on both sides of those, and they both hurt. But sometimes it's less clear. Sometimes one party pulls that childish, dick maneuver of deciding they want out and then being intentionally awful so the other person has to do the work of breaking up. It's cowardly and it sucks, but it happens.

One of my earliest high school breakups involved being ghosted. That was challenging because I was clearly the one being dumped but had to reach out and ask, "Hey, are you breaking up with me?" That's a blow to one's dignity. I committed to never being the kind of person who would mistreat someone just to make them do the leaving, and though I've never been a perfect partner, I think I've managed to keep that promise to all my exes. You, America, have 406 years of history of breaking almost every promise you've ever made to anyone. I know you don't like hearing that, but it's a fundamental fact you're going to have to come to terms with if you ever want to have a healthy relationship with anyone ever again.

So who is dumping whom in this case? On the surface, it looks like I am. I'm the one waiting to publish this letter until I'm safely on foreign soil. That sure smacks of ghosting. I feel this impulse to defensiveness, preemptively chaffing at accusations of cowardice. I need to sit with that, hold it, and acknowledge it. Maybe I am being cowardly. Maybe I should stay and fight for our relationship, America. Maybe I should stay and support you, play my part in your healing journey. But I don't believe that.

Here's the part in every breakup where I dredge up the history, the old grievances, and I know it's not flattering to need to put you down to justify my own actions, but this is just a part of the breakup process.

Back in 2020, beginning in the summer of George Floyd, I was involved in a lot of protesting, and I got on the radar of some very sick people. I don't hold you responsible for each of them, America. There will always be outliers, extremists. I'd received some ugly slurs before that summer (I'll never forget the first time someone responded to a blog post by calling me a "n---

-r lover"), and even some that verged on threats (pictures of cartoon characters pointing guns at the fourth wall with vaguely intimidating text), but that summer it felt non-stop, and it was really scary. One guy revealed he was a truck driver who lived out of state but regularly traveled through my town and threatened to drive my ex-wife off the road or run over my son. With some Facebook sleuthing by friends, we were able to figure out how he could see certain posts he referenced, then track back through relationships to discover his identity. I reached out to the FBI. They don't tell you what comes of that, but the individual stopped messaging me.

Another started sending these unhinged six-page rants to me and many of my coworkers, then moved on to management at the school district where I taught, telling them to fire me. I suspect it was the same individual who reported me to the state and had me investigated by the Teachers Standards and Practice Commission. I was cleared of his accusations of … burning down Portland, I guess? I never committed any crimes in my protesting there. I didn't even throw water bottles at the police or kick at the Feds' fencing because I found those kinds of tactics childish. But I think it's this same individual who still comes back every single week to downvote my YouTube show (a mild annoyance and an impressive demonstration of his commitment), and possibly the same person who wrote a letter to the local animal control accusing me of illegally letting my dog roam around off leash based on the evidence of a picture of my dog off leash *in my fenced backyard*.

Oh, and Tucker Carlson ranted about a list with my name on it to all his millions of viewers back when he was on Fox News. I'd signed a pledge to teach American history accurately. That produced its own wave of nasty-grams.

Mostly silly-season, small-bore stuff, right? But taken together, especially the guy who made the most specific death threats, had me really nervous around the time of Joe Biden's election in 2020. One night, when I was getting multiple threats from different sources simultaneously and I was alone in my house, I spiraled so badly I ended up pacing in my living room holding a loaded 9mm, thinking I might have to defend myself if someone came to the door. Ridiculous and embarrassing, I know, but also not good for my blood pressure.

I have a friend who worked, at the time, for the FBI. Once, as we were commiserating during the 2020 election, they confided that morale was already deeply wounded by the first Trump administration, and a lot of people were looking for the exits. I asked very directly if, in a second Trump administration, I would be able to call the FBI as I had before and expect them to investigate threats I received for speaking out against Trump's government. And this person told me I would basically be calling the Proud Boys for help. That was a turning point for me. I became convinced (and remain convinced) I will not be safe here during a second Trump administration.

Already, my harassers have started reminding me

they are still here. I received an anonymous postcard with "Your Body, My Choice" on the front (an alt-right rape threat popularized by professed white-supremacist Nick Fuentez), and a message on the back about how the "good guys won." Apparently, in today's United States, the good guys send anonymous postcards with rape threats.

And maybe anonymous threats are the extent of what they will do for the next four years. Or maybe, emboldened, they will believe they can do a lot worse. Not a safe country to live in.

And when I say "safe," I want to break that down a little. I don't mean "uncomfortable." There are times in any relationship where a person is uncomfortable. In fact, I'd go so far as to say one *ought* to feel uncomfortable at times, even in one's most intimate relationships, if those are going to be healthy. We have to have uncomfortable conversations. We need to disagree sometimes, and we need to talk that out. I used to spend hours debating issues with conservatives with whom I had (and still have) a great deal of respect. We disagreed about whether or not human beings are fundamentally good and can build communities out of those impulses, or fundamentally evil and need the constraints of law to keep them from descending into chaos. We disagreed about whether the United States should abide by the same values we expect of other countries or whether you, America, are exceptional in a way that means you get to treat other countries differently. These are big questions with significant ramifications, and the debates often got heated and sometimes personal. But we were always able to find our way back to shared values and mutual respect because we knew the other person was not saying, "You and millions of people like you are unworthy of fundamental human rights." I'm willing to acknowledge we came close to the line sometimes. When my conservative friends would try and argue for your exceptionalism, America, I would hear hints of the dehumanization of everyone else in the world. And I'm sure, when I tried to argue that their religious beliefs should not give them license to withhold healthcare or marriage from someone, they heard me treading on their fundamental right to their religions. It was uncomfortable. But it was never dangerous. And ultimately, those disagreements were valuable because they were illuminating even when they didn't result in agreement.

This is something very different, America. The people sending the death threats don't want to talk things through. But they're not the heart of the problem. It's you, America. You, the majority of you, decided a certain ideology rooted in hatred of others is acceptable. I know you have literally millions of different reasons why you made that choice. But can you honestly tell me you would simultaneously elect an ideology of hate and then say, "Let's keep it respectful. I'll keep you safe while you speak out"?

So maybe you're sending me away, and maybe I'm escaping you. In the end, it doesn't make much difference.

It's Not Trump.
Not Really.

America, you can't hide behind Donald Trump. This isn't really about him, and I think you know that. You can't say, "He's an aberration," and use that as an excuse. Yes, he's far outside the norm of your politics in terms of his behavior. But you like that, America. You want that. This is about you.

One of my best friends is a history teacher, and his primary area of expertise, America, is you. Flattered? You should be. My friend is amazing. Anyway, he taught me a concept that has helped me understand so many other elements of my relationship with you. He says we incorrectly teach history, and especially *your* history, using what he calls The Great Man of History. This theory dates back to the philosopher Thomas Carlyle in the 1840s, and according to my friend it still infects the way we understand the world. Carlyle said, "...the history of what man has accomplished in this world, is at bottom the History of the Great Men who have worked here. They were the leaders of men, these great ones; the modellers, patterns, and in a wide sense creators, of whatsoever the general mass of men contrived to do or to attain; all things that we see standing accomplished in the world are properly the outer material result, the practical realization and embodiment, of Thoughts that dwelt in the Great Men..." This is wrong in so many ways, and this lie skews our understanding of who we are, why we do what we do, and why we find ourselves in our current circumstances. How many late night dorm conversations revolve around the relative immorality of traveling back in time to murder Baby Hitler? Enough that the scene made it into the final montage of Deadpool 2. But once we abandon The Great Man of History mentality, we understand that if Hitler had been killed, the German people would have elevated someone similar. Maybe a little better. Maybe worse.

Here's an example of The Great Man of History myth: Do you know why we say the word "okay," America? You ought to know it because, not only is it a fundamentally American contribution to the language, it's one of your main exports, incorporated into a host of other languages around the world. It's also a great illustration of why the Great Man of History is a lie. If you ask a lot of people (including Google's new AI misinformation feature), they will tell you the origin of "okay" dates back to Martin Van Buren. See? A president. A "great man." It fits the model we want to believe is true. When Van Buren was young, his nickname was The Red Fox of Kinderhook because he was from Kinderhook, New York and had red hair. Then he got old. During his second run for the presidency (which he lost), some of his supporters started calling him Old Kinderhook because his hair was no longer red. And this, many will tell you, is where OK comes from.

But that's not true. The term already existed. It came about, much like modern internet memes, from a joke so obscure and confusing only a few people understood it even at the time. Here's the short version: A newspaper in Boston, Massachusetts ran a comedy piece making fun of a newspaper in Providence, Rhode Island. Boston had passed an ordinance making it illegal to ring dinner bells too loudly. A group of Bostonians thought this was silly, so they formed a satirical group to make fun of the law. The newspaper article, in an effort to make fun of the yokels in Providence, speculated about what a similar story might be like if carried in Providence. And in the satirical story of the real satirical group which did not really exist in Providence, most of the jokes, such as they were, involved spelling errors in the not-really-Providence newspaper. And at the end of the article, the imaginary editors of the newspaper being mocked used an abbreviation to say that the information in the not-real article was "All Correct." But because they were so stupid (according to the Bostonian humorist), they incorrectly abbreviated this as O.K.

Hilarious, right?

But the term caught on. It spread in the same way people have started saying LOL as a word. And then they started writing it as "OK" or "okay."

(Another incorrect attribution relates the term to the shooting at the OK Coral. Nope. That stood for Old Kindersley, the name of a livery that was down the street from where the shootout took place. It had nothing to do with Van Buren or Oklahoma [it's in Nevada] or the term "okay.")

See? We want to believe something is shaped by people we recognize (presidents, celebrity gunfighters), but it really comes from common people pushing up, not powerful leaders pushing down.

Or take something that may be even more American than "okay": Baseball. Americans really didn't like the idea that baseball may have been a variation of the British game of Rounders. They wanted it to be American. Fine. Maybe it is. But America, you want things to come from Great Men. So when a man named Abner Graves wrote a letter to a local newspaper falsely claiming that baseball was invented by a Civil War general, you ate that shit up. But General Abner Doubleday did not invent baseball. It was referenced in England as far back as 1672, and in Princeton, New Jersey in 1786, but both references imply it was already a common game, not some new invention. Abner Doubleday wasn't born until 1819, so unless he was such a Great Man that he not only served as a general in the Civil War but also invented a time machine, he did not invent baseball.[1]

Donald Trump hasn't invented shit, either. He's a two-bit conman who started life on third base, so his con is just a lot bigger than most. Like all con-men, he relies on distraction. America, you don't need to figure out Donald Trump. You need to figure out what he's distracting you from.

---

[1] Thanks to the podcast *Secretly Incredible Fascinating*, episode "O.K." for these two examples just when I needed them!

It's the Hate You Crave

Your racism has been around as long as you have, America. Not only does it predate your government, but arguably your government came into existence so that white, landholding men could make sure foreigners couldn't have too much say in the way they wanted to run their exploitative factories or plantations. The sexism, xenophobia, and racism has always been baked in. The "Great Men" didn't make those conditions, nor did they unilaterally change them to match their laudable values of equality and opportunity for all.

The leaders do not create the conditions that elevate them to leadership, and they can only steer a culture so

15

far once they have power. They are produced by a set of cultural conditions, and they mostly respond to those conditions. Trump didn't make you, America. You made him. And everything he has done or will do is a product of your encouragement or permission.

Donald Trump will die. I'm not threatening the man. He's a human being filled with McDonald's cheeseburgers. When he is gone, you will remain, America. And if you liked his rhetoric about kicking out immigrants and banning Muslims and grabbing women by their wherevers, someone else will step forward and say whatever it takes to give you exactly what you want. I'm not leaving because Donald Trump is making you a dangerous place. I'm leaving you because your choice of Donald Trump reveals you want to be a dangerous place.

But are you really going to be that dangerous? A lot of my friends and family have tried to convince me I'm overreacting. And all of their efforts make me even more worried. The only way you're going to get out of this is to take it very, very seriously, America. Ignoring an uncomfortable lump is not a cure for cancer. And "the news is too depressing, so let's not talk politics," will not save you from fascism.

The Law Will Not Protect You

For one thing, they assure me Donald Trump won't be able to do some of the things he's promised to do because those things would be against the law. Um, what? America, you elected a felon who told us he wanted to be a dictator. You made him the executor of all the federal laws, and those laws trump state laws. How do these people think laws work? I expect they are mixing up laws and their own sense that laws should be obeyed. The latter is not a law but a norm, and we should understand the difference.

The first Trump administration was a direct attack on

norms. Norms and laws overlap sometimes, but norms are those things most of us don't need to have enumerated and don't require to have explicit consequences imposed by the state. For example, it is a norm that men should not announce that they would like to date their daughters. It's not illegal to say that (on the radio, to millions of people, when being interviewed by Howard Stern), and it's even protected free speech as long as it's not a threat (though "date," when coming from an adjudicated rapist accused of raping, among other people, at least one of his former wives, is pretty clearly a threat to do something other than take her to the movies). But we all know we shouldn't say it. Most people would never consider saying it because they would find the idea itself abhorrent. But even the (hopefully) small minority who might think it wouldn't say it because it violates a norm.

I may not be an expert on much, but I have many years of experience working with children who experimented with violating norms to try to learn social boundaries. 14 year-olds often do things adults know to be socially unacceptable. Most of the time I found these could be dealt with by aiming a certain kind of glare which said, "I'm not commenting on this yet, but if you continue, I will speak about it, and your peers will know you have violated a norm. Do you want that conversation to take place?" It's an eloquent facial expression, finely honed by teachers and parents, and dramatically effective when employed properly. But it doesn't always work. Sometimes a kid will be genuinely surprised because they honestly didn't know they were violating a norm, and rather than making the quick calculation that their behavior produced the glare because a norm had been violated, they would look shocked and say, "What? What did I do?" At other times, kids who knew full well they had violated a norm would look shocked and say, "What? What did I do?" In either case, I would explain that their behavior was unacceptable because they are 14, even the ones who know better need to be reminded, and teachers can generally maintain better rapport with kids by giving those kids a chance to win rather than a chance to lose.

Occasionally a student, confronted about their norm-breaking, would double down a bit more, demanding to know which rule they were breaking. Time permitting, I could explain the difference between norms and rules. I once heard a story that the Prophet Muhammed said he never directly prohibited his followers from making soup out of camel dung precisely because he knew it would cause someone to try making soup out of camel dung. I have no idea if this story is true, but if so, it's a good illustration of the way norms don't need to be articulated, and that articulating them can even spur behavior which wouldn't have been considered otherwise.

We do have a catch-all rule which can apply if a student really wants to be difficult, but I'm loathe to employ it because it flies in the face of the most basic tenets of a law. We can prohibit any behavior which violates a teacher's explicit instruction and call it "insubordination." Insubordination is a very real rule. I could have been fired for insubordination by my employer, and I'm guessing the vast majority of you, America, could be fired for the same thing. (If someone is self-employed, as I am in my other job as a publisher of a small press, "insubordination" just becomes "dithering" or "indecisiveness." It still has consequences in the form of delayed decision-making and inefficiency, but it probably won't lead the employer to fire themself. I do encourage the self-employed to threaten to fire themselves from time to time. It keeps your employee on their toes.) My problem with insubordination isn't that it's unrealistic, but that it works in a way real rules and laws should not.

A rule of law, in contrast to a norm, should have four characteristics:

- A rule should be as clear as possible.
- A rule should not change unless absolutely necessary, and the change is understood by everyone.
- A rule should apply to everyone equally, including the people who write it and the people who enforce it.
- A rule should have a predictable consequence if violated.

A rule against insubordination violates all these characteristics. My students didn't know what, exactly, I was going to consider insubordination. They didn't know what I was going to tell them to do or not do tomorrow, so the rule was always changing. And unless I was going to hold myself accountable in some clear and public way for any inconsistency on my own part, and unless I had the ability to accuse and punish the school principal or superintendent for not obeying my classroom expectations, it's not a rule that's being enforced against everyone equally. It's barely a rule at all. It's a placeholder for maintaining a hierarchy of command.

Hierarchies all have these rules against insubordination. Even our military, which has a lot more rules than civilian life, operates with the understanding that orders from those of higher rank must be obeyed, while those of a lower rank cannot command those of a higher rank. This creates the danger of abuse, and all the branches have systems in place, with varying degrees of effectiveness, to make sure all the other rules and regulations are not demanded of those with a lower rank and ignored by those of a higher rank. The enforcement, to some degree, always comes from outside the direct chain of command. To a point. Somewhere, further up the chain, the enforcement arm is still an extension of the highest ranking officers. It is expected the generals will not employ their power to aim the enforcers only at the lower ranking but will allow themselves to be held accountable to the same rules. This can't be forced upon them. At the highest ranks, it's a norm, not a law.

America, like anyone who has worked with 14 year-olds, you've always had people poking and testing at your norms. Back in 1834, when the John Marshall Supreme Court ruled in favor of the Cherokee People in Worcester v. Georgia, President Andrew Jackson is reported to have responded, "John Marshall has made his decision; now let him enforce it." We don't know that he actually said that, but we do know Jackson ignored the ruling and sent troops to evict the Cherokee people, who were then forced to travel the Trail of Tears.

In the era of Trump, these violations of norms were less tragic but far more common, and only time will tell how consequential they will ultimately prove to be, because their effect is cumulative. A small violation creates a permission structure for the next. For example, it had become normal for presidential candidates to disclose their tax returns so voters could make a judgment about how honest they were and whether their financial dealings might create conflicts of interest voters should consider before casting a ballot. But there was no law. So Trump ignored it, and you permitted that, America. This made it a little easier for you to accept it when Trump violated the norm around Presidents revealing medical records from respected, legitimate medical professionals. If he didn't need to tell you about his financial health, and you decided that was fine, then he could find some joke doctor to say demonstrably false things about his physical fitness, and you were primed to accept that, also.

The next administration, I predict, will be all about challenging the norm that the enforcers should abide by the same laws as the enforced. America, you've decided that your recourse, when it comes to norm breaking, is not as important to you as mass deportation, harming (American) importers to (incorrectly) shift blame for inflation onto foreigners, and lowering taxes on the wealthiest oligarchs. This election was your last official, legal mechanism. Could the Republican Congress and Supreme Court (who have all hitched their wagons to Trump) stand up to him, block violations of the law, and impeach him? Technically, they could, I suppose. And Democrats could take back the House or Senate in a couple years. But even if they managed to take both and received enough support from the court Trump has created, will they be able to force him to abide by their decisions? To paraphrase the possibly apocryphal Jackson, "Let them enforce it."

Those who enforce the law are always in a tenuous position. We give them special permission to break some laws in order to enforce others based on the belief they will break laws for the benefit of the public and not for their own benefit. For example, a police officer can tackle someone who is attacking someone else. Tackling a person is assault. We allow the officer to violate not just the norm but the law itself, with impunity, because we believe they are committing that violation to protect the public. If we lose that faith, they become a gang of criminals who are immune from prosecution and can break the laws to benefit themselves simply because they are stronger, more numerous, and more heavily armed. From the inception of your police forces, America, you've blurred this line. The first police forces were slave patrols, breaking laws to preserve the legal framework of slavery. In many communities, the police still cannot be trusted to break the law for the benefit of the people they protect. The police claim they couldn't do their jobs if their immunity were removed, and that's probably true. But without the public trust, they also can't do their jobs. Not really. If we understand those jobs to be crime prevention or law enforcement (punishment), a police force which has lost public trust is now participating in violating the law. The norm that police should not break the law for their own benefit and should hold one another accountable from the bottom to the top of the organization must be preserved for the law to be enforced.

America, the person in charge of seeing that your laws are enforced is someone who breaks your laws, and not in ways that might be arguably in the interest of the public. Trump's crimes were all in his own self-interest. As if to make that point as clear as possible, Trump initially appointed Matt Gaetz to be the chief law enforcement agent in the United States, answerable only to the head of the Executive branch. Gaetz was about to be found in violation of House ethics rules by his own party for having sex with a 17 year-old. The only way to believe someone like Matt Gaetz will be bound by the norms necessary to enforce the laws is to believe he raped a child *for the benefit of the public*. Trump himself has been credibly accused, under oath, by at least one of his more than twenty accusers, of raping children. That's where you're at now, America. Those trying to comfort me that your laws will protect your people can only believe that if they think someone who rapes a child can be depended upon to only violate the law for the good of the public. And that's who you have chosen. Yeah, miss me with the idea that your laws should make me feel safe, America.

Self-Destruction is Not a New Habit for You

America, I know "gaslighting" is a term that's tossed around a lot in these breakup situations, so I'll avoid it, but lately you've shifted from telling me I'm being paranoid to telling me that I'll probably be okay because I'm a cishet white man living in a blue state, and I think that shift is worth discussing. Before, when I said we were on the road to fascism, you just told me I was crazy, that it could never happen here. I'm a bit more impervious to that dismissal than most people. I'm partly Jewish. My ancestors came over decades before the rise of the Nazis, in the early 1900s, so they weren't specifically fleeing an imminent genocide, but I'm sure they had friends and family who told them their home (probably in what is now Hungary) wasn't so bad, and they were crazy for leaving. I also know that all the members of that side of the family who didn't leave died in the camps. I understand people can't wait until every last person agrees it's time to go. That's too late. I know this truth in my DNA.

But you aren't even pretending that leaving is a bad idea anymore. You are promising mass deportations. And not just of those who are undocumented. I know most people don't understand how difficult your immigration system is. They hear "illegal" and think every undocumented person snuck across the border on foot. They don't understand the majority of people who are undocumented have merely overstayed their visas, and the majority of those come here by airplane. "Build the wall," right? A wall that will stop airplanes? A 40,000 foot tall wall? Anyone calling for a wall does not understand our immigration system or its challenges.

People get stuck trying to become naturalized citizens or green card holders because we have chosen to make the system prohibitively expensive. A friend of mine from Mexico had to pay more than $80,000 to become a citizen because, in addition to paying for lawyers, immigrants have to fund the courts, pay the attorneys arguing against them, pay the judges deciding their fates, and they don't get any of that back if they are found to have a valid claim. We don't do this is any other circumstance. When we want to dissuade people from making frivolous lawsuits, some states menace them with the threat of court costs if they fail, but we never say they have to pay the court costs if they *win*. Except in immigration court. There, they are always filing a frivolous lawsuit, because you, America, start from the presumption they are superfluous, worthless people.

But now you are talking about mass deportations of 20 million people. Those 20 million cannot possibly fund their own deportations. Even if you could steal the cost of their plane trips from their American bank accounts, they can't give you the money they would have injected into the economy, in the form of their labor and consumption, if they are gone. Migrant workers are a net gain for the economy, and you are going to take that away AND pay for the cost of hurting yourself. Times 20,000,000.

I don't think you've thought this through, and I don't think you really understand how many people that is. The high school where I taught has a thousand students. So a million people is a thousand of those medium sized high schools. That's twice the number of high schools in Oregon. So imagine all the high schools in Oregon and double it. Then twenty of those thousand high schools. Forty thousand Oregon high schools worth of people. Is that helpful?

The state of Oregon has only one maximum security penitentiary, and the population there is 1800 people. America, you are talking about more than ELEVEN THOUSAND state penitentiaries worth of holding facilities.

Oh, but it gets worse! By most estimates, there are only 13 million people who are undocumented. Who are the other 7 million people, America? If the 13 million undocumented people could be returned to their countries of origin (and they can't because their countries will not take them, but I'm sure you believe you could throw your weight around and make that happen), what about the other 7 million? That's almost four thousand Oregon State Penitentiaries worth of people, America. You already have the highest rate of incarceration of any country in the world, at over a million people in your jails and prisons. That's not just the highest rate, it's the largest total, larger than India and China which have much larger populations. You already spend $295 billion annually on funding your police, courts, jails, prisons, probation, and parole, and that's not even counting your immigration system (because, again, those costs are largely borne by immigrants themselves). Sure, $295 billion seems small compared to all your government spending at every level ($6.75 trillion), but it's more than four percent of all your current government spending. Imagine multiplying the number of people you're trying to incarcerate from 1 million to twenty-one. The costs are not simple multiplication. You will have to build that capacity. And, perversely, you'll have to do it at a time when your construction costs will be shooting through the roof precisely because you're imprisoning and deporting a lot of the labor force in the construction sector.

You are choosing to destroy your own economy,

America, and this may seem like something the world's wealthiest country would know enough to avoid, but it's actually completely in keeping with your character. Over and over you have made choices to harm yourself in order to hurt people of color, women, and the poor just a little bit more than you hurt yourself. Heather McGhee makes this case better than I ever could in her book *The Sum of Us: What Racism Costs and How We Can Prosper Together*. You really need to read that book, America. The way white communities chose to deprive themselves of beautiful public pools rather than share them with their Black neighbors; this is the microcosm for the way billionaires are going to choose to take a small hit to their own incomes, a minor inconvenience of a global depression, in order to create a world where they have very low corporate taxes and extreme control of every level of the government. Again, this isn't a trick you're falling for. This is you. This is what you recognized and wanted.

And this isn't me telling you this. Even if you think I'm way off base, you love Elon Musk. In a townhall on October 25th, he projected "temporary hardship" but said it is necessary to "ensure long-term prosperity." Whose hardship? Whose prosperity?

The markets seem to agree. These are the bets made by very wealthy people who are often wrong but are right often enough to stay wealthy. The initial market reaction after the election was exuberant on the stock side and anxious on the bond side. What does this mean? They believe Trump's tax cuts for corporations and the very wealthy are going to make them a lot of money in the short term. They also know Trump's tax cuts, combined with deportations and tariffs, are going to cause the prices of goods to go up and the national debt to balloon. If you break down the companies that did well in the early stock run up after the election, you can see that businesses that rely on foreign imports, like Volkswagen and Dollar General, took a hit. This isn't the opinion of some small town former high school English teacher. The people with the money know the combo is going to be very good for people who can cash out and park their wealth elsewhere, but that it's going to be bad for you, America. Bad for your consumers and bad for your debt.

So why would you possibly choose such a thing? Wouldn't even those elite, wealthy white men make more money in a healthy economy than in a cratering one? Yes, but not relative to the poorest, and that's how you roll, America. As you've done so often in the past, you are less concerned about lifting everyone up than you are about making sure the distance between the haves and the have-nots stays safely insurmountable. And you've done it the same way you always do: You've enlisted the have-nots in making sure it takes place.

Elon promises them hardships. They cheer for Elon at a hate rally in Madison Square Garden.

What I Worry Will Happen

As we've established, I'm just a small-town former high school English teacher who sometimes writes science fiction novels. As I used to teach students in my Science Fiction Lit classes, sci-fi authors are not prophets (with the possible exception of Octavia Butler), and we're not futurists. I don't know exactly how it will go. But I am making a huge bet (much larger, proportional to my net worth, than any stock or bond trader), that it's going to be really, really bad. Here's what I expect, America. Tell me I'm wrong. Please, make me wrong about all of this.

First, you'll start with small tariffs on all imported goods, and you'll start rounding up very targeted groups of immigrants. I'm betting you'll go for men from Latin America who have still not completed their naturalization process and have committed minor traffic offenses. No one will march for those men, and everyone will wait to see what the tariffs do to prices. And you, America, will pretend you don't care, but you will be listening very closely to see who speaks out. You'll be watching for every eye roll. You'll be keeping track.

When it's clear no one will complain too much about the increases in deportation, they'll start going after larger groups. They'll end the protected status for Haitians and force them into hiding or back to a country run by warlords. The political situation in many countries, not just Haiti but Mexico, Guatemala, Ecuador, and Venezuela will get worse due to an influx of returning former citizens, and if those countries experience the same kind of blame-the-migrants attitude you have employed lately, they will take a hard right turn as well, and they will stop accepting migrants. This will not stop you from rounding them up. After all, America, you have private prison lobbyists and fundraisers to pay back for their support, right? You'll build the "soft-sided facilities all over the country" they have been promising their shareholders in the run-up to this election.

Meanwhile, states and possibly even federal legislation will codify attacks on Trans people, making it illegal for them to participate in sports, use the bathroom, adopt children, and get married. And America, you will listen for the outcry and make sure it's not enough.

Then, under the guise of fighting pornography, you'll start making different kinds of depictions of those already-illegal Trans folx into criminal acts. And some people will speak out, but it's hard to do that without referencing what you're speaking out against, so their protests could, themselves, be deemed pornographic. If that silences the Trans advocates effectively, you'll move on to what Project 2025 calls "the LGBTQ agenda." Depictions of anything queer will be pornographic. A gay couple taking a family picture with their kids? Promoting the LGBTQ agenda. A Trans woman taking a selfie in women's clothes? Promoting the LGBTQ agenda. A book or TV show or movie with a gay love scene? And then one without a love scene, but with gay characters? What studio run by cishet white millionaires wants to risk making a multi-hundred-million dollar blockbuster that might get pulled out of the theaters and might even get some of them fined or jailed? They will comply in advance, censoring depictions of LGBTQIA+ people out of existence in the green-lighting, pre-production phase.

More and more states will pass more and more restrictive laws about women's healthcare. Some will ban abortion outright in every circumstance. Others will de facto ban it by making it impossible to get one. A national ban will probably be passed in the next couple years. The Supreme Court will uphold it. Maternal mortality will spike. In addition to these most tragic situations, there will be knock-on consequences, and I'm not just talking about the loved ones who will lose spouses and children and parents. One bit of speculation from one of my favorite pundits, Jamelle Bouie, is that while a lot of Republican rhetoric about the border seems to be about keeping people *out*, it may end up being about keeping people *in*. Abortion could provide the pretext to prevent people from traveling or moving resources overseas if the administrations' plans lead to economic catastrophe. If they are tanking the economy, they won't want that to be exacerbated by individuals relocating their assets. So they may say, in order to enforce the nationwide abortion ban, they need to prevent women from traveling or moving money to countries where they could get healthcare which is prohibited here. And then, surprise, you're all locked in.

The administration has also stated, explicitly, that they are going to try to circumvent the *Posse Comitatatus*. This is one of those places where a norm and a law overlap, but not perfectly. It is currently illegal for the military to participate in enforcing domestic policy inside the United States. But there are exceptions built into the law. A President can call up the military to help with disaster relief, for example, and while they are doing that, they can take action to preserve law and order, a responsibility usually reserved for law enforcement. That's legal, but the norm is that presidents won't employ that power willy-nilly because you, America, have historically been uncomfortable with the notion of armed soldiers patrolling your streets. But that could change. If the administration decides to declare our immigration situation is an "invasion" and a "disaster," will this Senate and House modify existing law to permit the military to operate within the United States at the President's discretion? Will this Supreme Court stop them? And once they are empowered to be used to round up undocumented immigrants, what will stop them from enforcing new mandates, like preventing women from traveling to receive healthcare, or preventing the LGBTQIA+ from existing publicly and thus "promoting the gay agenda"?

But you know what, America? It's not going to be just like what I imagine. It's going to be something else. Some weird left turn on a random Tuesday. It will be like Covid or Russia's attack on Ukraine, but not exactly like anything in the past. It will be China invading Taiwan or the Venezuelan government collapsing, except it won't be anything so predictable. Here's why sci-fi authors and futurists and gamblers always fail: Because nothing in the future is exactly like what is indicated by the past. Something else will come up which throws off all the calculations. And these new leaders, the ones you have chosen, will have to navigate those unforeseeable circumstances. And that's why I predict your kakistocracy will fare worse than the pundits expect. The op-ed writers have to write weekly columns where paragraph two provides evidence for paragraph one and flows seamlessly into paragraph three. But the world doesn't work that way. And when the unpredictable happens, the people in charge have to respond. Maybe they will respond in unpredictable ways, too. Maybe these people who are grossly unqualified to do anything except their one core competency, kissing the ass of the boss, will turn out to suddenly care about their own legacies and the people they are supposed to serve, and they will handle the unforeseeable in impressive ways. That would be great. But not only are you not planning on that, America: You don't even want that. It would actually fly in the face of the mandate you've given the leaders you've picked. They would be betraying you if they were competent. You have demanded chaos and oppression as entertainment. When shit hits the fan, you picked these people because you don't really want someone who will clean it up.

That's why I think it will be much messier than anyone predicts. The messes will compound. The usual cleaners will be cowed to silence. And the majority will revel in their own filth.

And that's still not the worst part.

The Thing that Scares Me the Most

Here's what scares me most, America. (I mean, the things that scare me the most are sharks, but that's completely irrational and not relevant.) It's not concentration camps, though those will be terrible. It's not women dying in hospital parking lots, though that will be terrible. It's not LGBTQIA+ folx having their marriages dissolved, their families destroyed, going back into the closet, and losing their lives because of Project 2025 attacks, though that will be terrible. It's not seemingly decent people revealing they were hateful, and caring people being scared into callous silence. These outcomes are all so awful, it's hard for the most privileged of us to imagine anything worse.

But none of these things are new. You've thrown immigrants and your own citizens in concentration camps before, America. You've killed women rather than let them make their own choices. You've pushed LGBTQIA+ folx into the closet or into the grave. You've let your worst people take their masks off, and you've made your best people pretend they don't notice and then live with the guilt for the rest of their lives.

And that's what scares me most, America. It's that after this ends, whether that's in four years or a decade or a half a century, you'll do that thing you're so good at. You'll decide to forget. You'll say, "Whew, boy, that Trump period was sure awful. Glad that guy is gone. And all the people who participated, either actively or passively, well… that was just 'economic uncertainty,' I guess. Groceries were expensive. Russia was misbehaving. That's why it all happened. Glad we've put it behind us." And here's why that is the worst possible outcome, America. Because the only thing worse than a rape is ignoring it so it can be two rapes. The only thing worse than slavery is pretending it wasn't so bad and instituting slavery again. The only thing worse than a genocide is forgetting and allowing another genocide.

Many of my closest friends and family who have been the most supportive have said, "We understand why you're going, and we know you're doing the right thing. It's only for four years, and then we'll see you again." I understand where this is coming from, and I love them for their optimism and desire to see me happy and whole and back with them. But the "four years," ironically, reminds me exactly why I don't think it will be only four years. If they think this is a problem of a presidency now, that may be the excuse they hold onto at the end of that presidency, and holding onto that lie will not make you a safer place in four years, America.

America, most of your people's love for you, their superficial, flag-waving patriotism, is rooted in this lie; that you are a good, moral nation who has committed infrequent, small lapses. This lie is so ingrained, you have a visceral reaction when anyone dares to countermand it. The rare gimlet-eyed, honest leader may nod toward reality with some anodyne version of, "We might not have always been perfect," or "we may not have always lived up to our ideals," but even this makes many audiences sneer. It doesn't inspire you like the lie, America. You demand worship. You want to be reminded that you are good and just. And the worse you behave, the more you want your leaders to say, "Everyone over on the other side is terrible, and maybe they are even most of America, but America is perfect and good." I'll bet, if it were possible to create a kind of graph of the worst things you've ever done, ranking them on some impossible axis of immorality, and then you created a similar timeline of increases and decreases in the number of flags flying on front porches, the graphs would line up pretty well. Japanese internment? Lots of American flags. Headed off to kill 150,000 Iraqi civilians and displace a million more in a country that had no involvement in the 9/11 attacks? Lots of flags flying. Devising a system to rip babies from their mothers' arms just so other people would hear how horrible we're being and choose not to exercise their legal right to apply for legal asylum? Better get a bigger truck to fly an even bigger flag.

I do love you, America. Maybe that's mostly a function of identity, a sense that who I am is so tied up in you that if I dared to stop loving you, I wouldn't know myself. This is what keeps a lot of people in abusive relationships, and I'm sure I'm not immune. I'm willing to acknowledge I sound like many beaten spouses when I say: There's a lot about you to love, America. I love your land. The Grand Canyon, Niagara Falls, the dense forests of the Pacific Northwest where I've made my home, the striking vistas of Alaska or the Badlands of Wyoming, but also the fields of corn and soybeans flashing by when I drive through Iowa or the desolate deserts of west Texas and the swamps of the Gulf Coast. I've traveled to every one of your states, and I love your natural beauty. I love your diversity, the number of languages I can hear when I walk the streets of San Francisco or New York or LA or Chicago. I love your art, your music, your food. And I have loved the life I've been lucky enough to have here. I have served the public for 24 years, and people have been so good to me. The students in my classroom, the colleagues in my buildings, the parents in my community, the church congregations of my childhood, total strangers on trains and subways and airplanes, in truck stops and taxis and late night diners. Please don't misunderstand; it *will* break my heart to leave you, America, not the first day when I will be filled with relief, but over and over when I notice all the ways every other country is not my home. I will miss you in ways I cannot predict.

I can love you without believing the lie, America. And so could all your people. Better yet, they could choose a new way to love you. They could acknowledge the lie and learn to love you not for your moral perfection or even in spite of your "small lapses," but because of the way you could bravely look yourself in the mirror. It could be a source of incredible national pride to undertake the hard work of fully acknowledging that this is who you are, and deciding to change, to pay the reparations to the people you can pay and mourn the ones you can never repay. To sit with shame and figure out how to build a country that will never commit those crimes again. Wouldn't that be a more powerful form of patriotism, America? To love you for the way you were brave instead of loving you for the country you're not and never have been? Maybe you could choose that, someday. Maybe your people could gift that kind of patriotism to themselves and their children. But it will not be the work of the next presidential election or any single election, and as long as people think an America without Trump will be a healed America, you will never fully heal.

The Democrats Will Not Save You, and No Third Party Will, Either

The punditocracy has been spilling ink about the ways the Democratic Party should change itself to regain power, and the leaders within the party have been sharing their thoughts, too. These do not make me hopeful, America. They make me more convinced things are going to get much worse before they get better.

One of the theories is the Democratic Party needs to win elections by adopting more of the values of the Republican Party. They don't come right out and say this, most of the time. They say Democrats should concern themselves less with identity, with "woke-ness," with "language policing." Note the subtext: Democrats shouldn't spend energy concerning themselves with the issues of minority groups, shouldn't call out racism and sexism. Imagine they took this advice. Will you be healthier, America, if both parties agree to let more people be ignored, more people be discriminated against, more people be harmed?

Some say Democrats need to become much tougher on immigration. Is this really the message any Democrat should be hearing as the Republicans fire up their mass deportation machine? Join in now to regain power?

Some say the Democrats were doomed by global inflation and are merely faring just as poorly as incumbent administrations around the world. This is simultaneously true and unhelpful. While inflation was certainly a huge factor for many voters, and while trying to convince people the pain they are feeling isn't so bad because it's worse everywhere else is a losing strategy in terms of persuasion, if the Democrats take this lesson, they will A) not feel a lot of impetus to change, and B) fall into the old trap of dismissing white supremacy and patriarchy as functions of economic anxiety. If people are feeling anxious about the price of eggs, and that inclines them to choose to take one neighbor's healthcare, split up another neighbor's marriage, and deport a third neighbor, the problem isn't the price of eggs! The problem is that you, America, needed so little motivation to be so hateful.

I worry the Democrats are going to learn exactly the wrong lessons: Don't nominate women or people of color. Don't choose to keep unemployment down, but next time allow mass unemployment to quickly reduce inflation. Tolerate more racism and sexism in your own ranks to win over more sexist and racist voters. These may all be means to gain power. None of them are strategies to make a better country.

I recognize an establishment party can't simply forego winning in order to hold onto values. They are an election-winning machine. The machine broke this time, and they are trying to fix it so it can do what it's supposed to do, not build a completely different device which loses elections but promotes democratic values. But I hope they learn the lesson from the turn-out more than the lessons from the exit polling. Yes, many voters told them they cared about inflation more than anything. But all those exit polling respondents were people who voted. The bigger lesson should come from the enthusiasm gap which is evidenced by the lower-than-expected Democratic turnout and the higher-than-expected Republican turnout. The Dems just weren't the party with the exciting platform. And there's a good reason for that. They chose not to be.

For the last three elections, progressives and conservatives have flipped on the fundamental question of change. When Reagan-era conservatism was in its intellectual infancy, William F. Buckley Jr. described it best. He said conservatives are the ones who "stand athwart history and cry, 'Stop!'" As I've argued frequently, much to the surprise of some of my more conservative friends, I think this kind of conservatism is incredibly valuable ... if that were truly what it were all about. In her novel *Go Set a Watchman*, Harper Lee had her character Atticus Finch describe this as the brakes on the airplane, and the progressives are the wings. We *do* need both to work well. We need people who will push the country forward, and we need more cautious people to say, "Slow down. Let's think about the unintended consequences of those changes and not go too fast." Only, let's not forget the same novel reveals Atticus Finch was a member of the KKK. The kind of conservatism William F. Buckley Jr. described should have been the less sexy, less dramatic, generally losing platform most of the time. But it wasn't. Because the animating force beneath it was always racism and misogyny. Conservatives were crying "Stop," because they didn't want women and people of color to have increased power in society, and it turns out you, America, can get very excited about a person saying, "I promise no change" if that was a dog whistle for, "I will protect your more privileged position in society."

Now, as Ezra Klein points out in *Why We're Polarized*, for decades the wealthy elites of the Republican Party used racism as fuel to get poor whites to vote for tax cuts for the wealthy. But (to mix metaphors) they built a machine they couldn't control, and at some point the check was bound to come due. Those elites lost control of the party, and it really did become a party of radical regressivism, a party so backward-looking it literally branded itself with the slogan, "Make America Great Again." All that "keep my privilege" energy was harnessed, and it was unconstrained by the boring platform of "keep free market economics." The Republican establishment did their best to hold onto the tail of the stampeding elephant just to get more tax cuts for the rich, but that wasn't the party's primary focus anymore. The Republicans had become the party of radical change, and that radical change was in the direction of reverting back to some '50s world of legal spousal abuse and de facto legal lynchings.

Meanwhile, for the last three elections, the Democrats have been the party of the status quo, a role progressives don't know how to play very well. Playing defense against charges of radicalism by the far more radical party, they have said, "Scared of a Black man as President? Here's a beer summit to show you it's not scary because we aren't going to do anything real to address racism." And, "Scared of having taxpayer funded free healthcare? Here's a messy half-fix." And, "Scared of unnecessary foreign wars but also scared of messy retreats? How about drone wars and quagmires that don't make the front page?" And, "Scared we're not tough enough on immigrants? We'll deport even more of them than the Republicans, and that way you'll trust us to maintain border security." This is not to say the Democrats haven't had some significant accomplishments. It's just that they have worked very hard to temper them, either in the laws themselves or in their rhetoric about the accomplishments, so they wouldn't scare people into thinking they wanted to make too much change too fast. The Democrats became the brakes on the plane because the Republicans became huge engines pushing the airplane backwards.

Notice the pattern in all the Democrats' choices. Fear. They are afraid of scaring people. This is endemic to progressivism. Those desiring to make change are afraid responsible conservatives will say, "Slow down. Let's think about this," because that's precisely what functional conservatism *should* be saying. Cautious progressives are behaving like cautious progressives. But that shouldn't put them in the position of defending the status quo. The reason that's happening is that small-c conservatism is dead and has been replaced by MAGA extremism.

Rightwing fascist movements are not afraid of scaring people. Fear, pain, and blame are the fuel of fascism. And fascism is not a governing ideology. It's a movement to gain power, not to produce solutions. In fact, solutions are anathema to the project. If a fascist government makes the lives of its people better, the people motivated by fear of the other, by a desire to cause pain to the blamed, will not be motivated. Fascism gains power by making people scared and angry, then directing their fear and anger at someone to harm. Once in power, fascism stays in power by actively working to make everyone's life worse so the anger towards the blamed group is constantly dialed up.

Each time the right takes power, they can do scarier and scarier things. Each time the left is in power, they do smaller and smaller things to course-correct. Take, for example, ICE. The U.S. Immigration and Customs Enforcement has been such a significant element of our politics over the last decade, many people presume it's a department that has existed for as long as you've been a country. The employees on Ellis Island processing waves of European immigrants were ICE agents, right? Wrong. ICE has only been around since 2003. A whole bunch of the design of our immigration system is fundamentally racist (country quotas being the most obvious example), so it's easy to see the people who are simply trying their best to work in a broken system as villainous, but the agency is young and operates at the whim of the Executive branch. Now, in a functional push-pull between conservatives and progressives, a progressive administration would examine the data and come to the conclusion that you, America, need a lot *more* immigrants. Immigrants contribute to the economy, commit fewer crimes than native born citizens, and compensate for your low birth rate. A truly progressive administration would be devising systems to expedite access to immigration courts, seek out global talent, and do away with country quotas which are a terribly inefficient (and racist) way to decide who will make the best impact on a country.

Then, a functional conservative response would be to say, "Slow down," to reduce the rate of immigration, to test those systems for efficiency, and to evaluate the unintended consequences of waves of immigrants moving into communities which may have lacked the capacity to absorb immigrants for specific reasons. Maybe some places need more housing. Maybe others need more English-as-a-second-language teachers in their schools. Maybe some need beefed-up medical infrastructure because they were designed around a decreasing birth rate and now have an increasing one. A functional conservative government would say, "Let's slow this influx until we can improve capacity, and let's let the private sector catch up so this doesn't require massive expenditure by the government." And this could be a reasonable debate informed by the severity of the situation. Voters might say, "The growth isn't such a big problem that it needs to be slowed. Let's stick with the progress for now." Or they might say, "Yeah, we're uncomfortable with the unintended consequences manifesting in our community. Let's give conservatives power to slow this and make it more effective."

But we don't have that kind of debate at all because we have a regressive, fascist movement saying demonstrably false and racist things about "invasion" and "hoards" and "vermin" and a tepid progressivism that can't push back and say, "That's a lie, a racist lie, and here's why we need to improve the system to increase immigration."

So the Democrats under Obama deported even more immigrants than under Trump. Did that convince anyone the Democrats were the party to trust on immigration? No. Because they aren't. A party with principles would be pushing against the lie that immigration is bad, not adopting the presuppositions of the right and trying to present themselves as the slightly less frightening version.

I understand the reply from Democrats that they can't fight every battle and need to prioritize. That's why they devoted so much energy to changing the healthcare system and let immigration slide further rightward under Obama, and it's why Biden preserved the closed-border status of the pandemic lockdowns far after lifting pandemic restrictions in every other area of our lives. Immigration wasn't the priority. But they didn't just cede the issue, they gave up on having a distinct articulation of the problem, so their policy prescriptions, no matter how draconian they were in practice, looked like weak, mealy-mouthed versions of the Republican efforts because Democrats couldn't articulate why they would do anything differently.

If the lesson the Democrats learn from this election is that they should be more cautious or more inclusive of MAGA ideology, they will continue to try to be something other than the wings lifting the plane forwards. They are bad at being brakes, and you, America, are really screwed if they just add more jet fuel to the engines going in the wrong direction.

Some, seeing this breakdown, naturally hope a third party will be a solution. It would be fantastic if we could have multiple viable, functional options. Those who say the US is a two party system, as though that's a *fait accompli,* are forgetting that a system can be changed. But there are four reasons why third parties aren't going to save you anytime soon, America.

First, they lack the infrastructure to be viable, and most don't even care. A third party that was committed to making real change, to passing legislation that would make a difference in the lives of voters, would build out a complete electoral apparatus, running candidates in local and state elections and devoting resources to building those up first, then showing legislative results, and then building on those. Third parties devoting their resources to presidential runs every four years are telegraphing they aren't serious about governing, because even if some long-shot candidate were to win, they wouldn't have seats in the House or Senate and would end up being beholden to the two parties they ostensibly ran against.

The second reason third parties will not save you from your fascist inclinations, America, is that institutions exist to preserve themselves. This is a nearly-universal law of politics rooted in human biology. We don't want to go away. We don't want the organizations we make to go away, either. What this means for third parties is that, even when they clearly have ideologies which are more closely aligned with one of the major parties or the other, they will put their own self-preservation above ideology. Parties are election-winning machines. If they can't do that, they are useless. So third parties will always run against the party they might beat, and that means they are going to peel off votes from the party closest to themselves. In some places that would be fine. By all means, please build out a strong, more progressive party in a dependably Democratic city where the

Democrats are not serving the people's interests effectively, and please create a truly conservative option (yes, one that is far more conservative than I would ever be comfortable with, but truly conservative) in some locality where the Republican Party isn't serving the needs of the residents. And then build from there. But those interested in third parties (mildly interested. Willing to vote for them every four years but not willing to do the day-to-day work to make them viable) should not be surprised when they hear their campaigns dismissed as "spoilers." They are. That's just a fact. If a third party doesn't want to be peeling off votes from a hegemonic major party, it has to build itself up to be a hegemonic major party.

The third reason third parties won't save you, America, is because the people to whom third parties most appeal are people who, by the very nature of their votes for a third party, are telegraphing that they are not as interested in compromising to build coalitions as they are in maintaining purity. You, America, are not bound to have two parties forever. You could have three or five or twenty. More ominously, you could have one party very soon. But you will never have a party which can make significant changes to improve people's lives if it is not interested in building coalitions. And yes, that does involve uncomfortable compromises. And yes, too much compromise can lead to a group (or an individual) losing their identity and purpose. It's not easy to figure out how much compromise one can live with.

But the first three reasons might all be moot, America,

or at least they are trumped by the fourth. A third party will not save you from fascism because fascism is what you want. For all the usual (and justified) dissatisfaction with the Democratic Party, they didn't lose the election because they ran an uninspiring candidate or had unpopular policies or faced stiff competition from more popular third parties. They lost because even with policies the vast majority of Americans claimed to like, a candidate who ran a remarkable campaign in a short period of time, hitting all her marks and never making any big gaffes, she still underperformed a felon and adjudicated rapist with vague policy proposals that included many highly unpopular ideas. That didn't matter. And while I'm sure her race and gender scared off some voters, they were probably a push since they reassured and motivated others. You would elect a woman, America, if she promised to reinforce the patriarchy inherent in fascism. You wouldn't elect Barack Obama right now, but you might elect a Black man if he promised to maintain and strengthen white supremacy. The election of America's first Black president woke you up, America. You might not like the word "woke," but that's really what happened. It's just that instead of "woke" being the AAVE term for awakening to the realities of systemic racial injustice, the majority of Americans, crossing racial, religious, and gender lines, were activated during Obama's presidency to the fact that our hierarchy could change, and they decided they desperately wanted to go backwards.

America, you might not be able to pinpoint which

"Great Again" you want to return to, and whatever year you would choose would certainly not have been great for most of your people, but the majority of your people are in agreement that backwards and to the right towards something in history (just not your own history) sounds better than a future without the hierarchy they've come to depend upon.

All the criticisms of the Democratic Party, and all the efforts to create a third option, should be viewed in this context: If you, America, are so far gone that you would choose a felon and rapist who holds a hate rally in Madison Square Garden, it's really not the fault of the Dems or anyone criticizing them from the left. Even if the Dems had been perfect and all the Leftists had been satisfied, you don't want what they are selling, America. And until you decide this whole electing-people-who-revel-in-causing-harm-instead-of-solving-problems thing is not working out for you, the Democrats or third parties won't be able to save you from yourself.

Caution, Meet Wind

America, you may find this surprising, but all my life I have been small-c conservative when it came to my personal decision-making. Decades ago, in college, I fantasized about really going for it, living on a shoestring, maybe even riding the rails like some cartoon hobo, and trying to make it as a writer. Instead, I fell in love with the safe girl who seemed to love me back (twenty years later she confessed she never really loved me, probably in part because I was too boring and safe). I got what I thought would be a safe job. Teaching! No danger there, right? I bought the house I could afford, then the next house I could afford. I started a small publishing company, but I made sure it never had any debt, so some years it made a thousand dollars and some years it lost it, but it couldn't ever really take off because I didn't devote enough time or resources to make it a wild success or a wild failure. I paid my taxes and voted for them to be increased every time so I could live a quiet life in a nice community with a library and a museum and good-enough public schools rather than hoard my tax money to live in a miserable place where I was slightly wealthier than the other miserable people around me. I never went big, America. I chose a little life.

At one point, believe it or not, I considered running for public office. I love politics and had this naive notion I could write legislation that would help people, maybe even help you, America. But I also had this competing erroneous belief that you would never vote for a funny-lookin' bald guy with imperfect teeth who was an agnostic and believed in working for the public good ("Socialist!"). Up until then, to paraphrase Sting, I'd only seen politicians who looked like game show hosts. I had the two most important characteristics you require, America: I'm white and male. I'm also cis and straight, but those aren't selling points, just hurdles I don't have to overcome. For you, the whiteness and maleness are significant advantages. But it seemed being a Christian was also essentially required. Silly me. We all know better now. Being a Christian in the sense of the word that I was taught in my childhood is actually a huge hurdle. But being a Christo-fascist (or being a non-Christian who is willing to carry water for Christo-fascists) is essential. I wasn't willing to pretend to be a Christian. So I never took the risk.

I self-censored my own books, always imagining some angry parent coming before the school board to read some quotes out of context to try to get me fired. Again, the joke is on me. One of the people who ended up trying to get me fired used, as his main justification, a picture of me holding a Black Lives Matter sign standing next to my wife who was wearing her guillotine earrings. He didn't point to the sign in that letter. Instead, he said that her earrings meant I was calling for the mass slaughter of my students ala the French Revolution. I'm not even kidding. He demanded I be fired because of my wife's earrings. Good thing I pulled my punches in the novels he didn't read, right?

Late in life, I finally tried taking some small gambles. I ran for higher office in my statewide union on a platform that we should spend our energy preparing to engage in statewide strikes. The members said that was a little too scary and voted for a nice guy who they knew wouldn't change anything too much.

I took a big financial gamble, taking out a second mortgage on my house to help fund my company and my wife's. That turned out to be poorly timed. The investment in her company is a total loss if we walk away from you now, America, so we're headed off with nothing but my meager savings.

And you know what? I'm kinda' starting to feel okay with that. Sure, it's terrifying. I'd much rather be leaving with a nice, comfortable financial cushion we could use to put down roots in some other country. But that's just not the situation in which we find ourselves. Like so many people leaving toxic relationships, I'm walking away with the clothes on my back, and in a way, that's exciting. You are forcing me to become the person I dreamt of being thirty years ago, the vagabond writer, and maybe, just maybe, that will turn out to be for the best. I will have the time to devote to the authors I have committed to publish, and I'll be able to write. More importantly, when I write, I won't have to worry about what some newly activated, anti-woke denizens of alt-right message boards might do to me. And that's going to be key for me.

You see, America, people are learning how they are going to fight back. Some are planning to take to the streets, and I hope they are learning about organizing, because it's not something that happens spontaneously. It's a lot of work. Some people already have those skills, and others have natural aptitudes in the area and will demonstrate they are willing to learn. I believe in those people. I also know street protests are just a part of a bigger movement. By themselves, street protests get attention and unite people, but they don't make change. But if the attention drives other action (like making legislators change votes because they fear losing the support of their constituents), street protests could play a vital role, especially if they are employed early when the new regime thinks no one cares. The earlier the action, the more it will matter.

And there will be a lot of other kinds of action. One

important kind of resistance, especially when consequences for speaking out get more dangerous, will be quietly gumming up the works. If people don't have the numbers to mobilize around a "you can't arrest us all" message and aren't willing to say, "go ahead and arrest the few of us" (not judging. That's really hard), then one of the best ways to fight back will be to have civil servants (and the employees of corporations collaborating with the regime) who push the envelope by slow-playing their own work and sabotaging efforts to carry out the regime's goals. A person might not be able to volunteer to take a bullet, but sometimes saying, "Sorry, sir. I guess I forgot to complete the paperwork to order those cattle cars. Guess we can't pick those detainees up today," may be a lot more productive than an act of dramatic self-sacrifice. America, some people are going to stand up to you just by being pains in your ass.

One thing that anti-fascists often recommend is focusing on the skills you already have rather than trying to develop all the skills you might need to fight back. No one is Rambo. Be glad because John Rambo was a deeply unwell individual. No one is John Wick. Be glad because his life has been very sad, and a cool suit does not make up for that. No one is John McClane, and that's good because the fight against fascism is not going to be won in a night. Some people have medical training. Some people are good at connecting with others in ways that aren't easily tracked. Some people might not be able to reveal their faces in a protest, but that could mean they won't have a record when they need to drive a person across state lines for healthcare.

And yes, America, there will be some people who just punch Nazis. Do I like that we live in a world where some people need to be punched? No. But I like it a lot better than a world where Nazis walk around not being punched. And America, until you're ready to create a culture where it's so socially unacceptable for anyone to be a Nazi that the Nazis can't build a movement, we're going to need people who let them know they don't own the streets. I know you don't like anti-fascists, America. There's a really easy way to make anti-fascism irrelevant. Reject fascism! If you can't figure out how to do that, America, there's going to be punching.

I'm too old to be punching people anymore, America. And I'm too loud to be the person who quietly gums up the works. I made a choice, years ago, to be one of the people at the antifa protest who didn't have a mask on. I respected the people who wore masks, and they (mostly) respected that I was not going to break laws, was going to use my real name, and was going to be a public voice. We understood that some people, due to skin color and body type and visible disabilities, might never be able to hide their identities, and others might, and some of us could choose, and we respected one another's roles, just as we respected the medics and the ACLU observers and the journalists, because we knew it was going to take a lot of different people doing different things to make change.

And we knew we might not succeed. People of Color

understood this better. It's harder for white people, and even harder for white men, to accept that some things might be outside of our control. That's just not in our training. When confronted with things outside our power, we diminish their importance or ignore their existence. But America, I think what's going to happen to you over the next few years is going to be very hard to diminish or ignore. (Maybe white guys will not demand to be the leaders of every effort to push back, but I'm skeptical.) We're going to need to learn to respect one another's roles, and we're going to need to learn to accept our own limits if any person of conscience is going to figure out how to push back against you in the future you're now facing.

My Role and My Limits

And that's why I'm leaving you, America. That's my role. To be your ex. Your exile. (I imagine this written X-ILE in the font of the X-Men, because I'm a giant nerd). As anyone who has ever become an ex has learned, it's not an identity one can inhabit. We were a we. I cannot be a not-we. I will take this opportunity to learn about who I am when I'm not a part of you.

This is not going to be easy. The grass is not always greener, and no matter where I land, I know I'll be in a country with its own problems. I will be an outsider, so I won't be able to have much impact on solving those problems, and I know my ability to have much of an

Benjamin Gorman

impact on you, America, probably ends here. Sure, I will be able to comment on things from afar, and maybe some people will find that perspective useful, but I will be much easier to dismiss by your people. And that's legitimate. The people on the ground should be the experts. I have ceded that. As much as I love politics, my ability to make a positive political impact will be reduced to conversations with friends and family, and to offering a helping hand to my new neighbors in whatever way they would appreciate without stepping on toes. I believe helping a neighbor is an important political act. I will still be able to do that. And maybe that will be enough to let me rest easy knowing I did what I could before I left you, America.

Sometimes, I expect, I will be deeply sad. Maybe some of that sadness will be regret, but even if I'm reassured I made the right choice every time I read the news, that won't be a source of joy. You will haunt me after this breakup. Your impact on every other country in the world makes you inescapable, and if I'm even half-correct about how bad things will get for you, the consequences for every other country in the world will be dire. You'll remind me of your presence every day, like the ex who keeps showing up on a Facebook or Instagram feed, only multiplied by a few hundred million. You will be on my mind when I don't want to think about you. I know that. I've had that experience after breakups before.

And I'm sure the anxiety about future regrets will wane. (We really need a word for that feeling. Maybe one already exists in German. Anxiety about future regret.) I'm sure I'm not the only one who experiences that sensation. I've felt it intensely after a few breakups, especially when I was the person ending them. I'm ashamed to admit that more than once I've reached out to exes and asked them if I made a terrible mistake. Luckily those women had the wisdom and strength of character to know that a person who would break up with you once isn't a person you want to trust with your emotional wellbeing again. I regret ever having put them in the position to reconsider, though. That was unfair to the point of cruelty, and it's not really the kind of mistake you can apologize for without revisiting it to make it worse. I hope, America, that I've learned from those experiences and the wisdom of some of my exes. Because there may come a time when you reach out to me, in some way, to invite me back into a relationship with you. It may be through something impersonal and bureaucratic. I could end up not being permitted to remain in some other country and needing to return. Or it could be about my parents' health, or my brother or sister needing me back for whatever reason. But that's not how we'll rekindle a healthy relationship, America.

I've given it some thought, and I think I can articulate what it would take for me to come back. This is an unhealthy mental exercise, I know. I've done this to myself before, wondering what it would take for me to reenter a relationship when it was clear the other person didn't want me back, anyway. Maybe it's just part of the grieving process, or maybe it's vanity, holding onto the possibility it would ever come to pass in order to protect my own ego. Regardless, here's what I think I would need in order to feel comfortable getting back together with you, America:

- Do you make consenting adults feel safe to love who they love, kiss who they kiss, have sex with who they have sex with, marry who they marry, raise kids with who they want to raise kids with? It's not enough to merely allow people to do these things, America. Do you let them know you'll defend their freedom to be themselves in relationships?

- Do you honor racial differences, or do you still tell people you are reluctantly willing to ignore their skin color or culture as long as they do all the same things white people do plus spend their energy projecting their commitment to whiteness?

- Do you recognize that vast wealth inequality is a danger to everyone, or do you still think any effort to close the wealth gap is a move towards oppression?

- Do you recognize the vast difference between being a country where a majority of the people are Christian and being a Christian country? Do you honor people's rights to have their own faiths or no faith at all, or do you still try to impose elements of the majority's religion on everyone else through official or de facto official acts?

I know it's absurd to tell you how to change as I'm walking away, America, but if you'll indulge me further, consider this: You can't just make one of these changes or make them one at a time because systems of oppression reinforce one another.

Intersectionality

America, as long as you have white supremacists, they will use gender and sex as means to maintain a racial hierarchy. White supremacy in this country always used gender and sex, depicting men of color as threats to white women and white men as protectors of subservient, domesticated, weak, passive women who couldn't possibly be liberated from the "protection" of white men because of the danger they faced from men of color. Anything that challenged the strict gender binary, whether it was gay relationships or individual trans identities, was a challenge to the gender roles necessary to preserve the racial hierarchy.

But the racial hierarchy served to protect the class hierarchy as well. While slavery is the most obvious example because it was so violent and morally repellent, there are plenty of examples of this in the North and in your post-slavery history, America. As I'm sure you're well aware, the geography of New York City was very intentionally designed by the wealthy to pit racial groups against one another, cordoning off racial groups into districts which would be policed by (then non-white) Irish immigrants to maximize interracial violence and state-sanctioned violence in a very intentional effort to maintain the power of WASPs who pulled the strings. This manifests differently in other cities, but the fundamental impetus is the same: employ racial divisions to preserve wealth inequality.

Another example of this intersection of racism and wealth inequality was the murder of Michael Brown which ignited the political unrest in Ferguson, Missouri in 2014 (and again on the anniversaries of his murder in 2015 and 2016). The common, personalized understanding of the cause of the political unrest is that a white police officer, Darren Wilson, shot and killed Michael Brown, an 18 year-old Black man. The officer claimed he killed Brown in self defense and was acquitted for the murder. The people of Ferguson responded, first with peaceful protests, then, when attacked, with violent protests.

If a person examined this story through this purely personal lens and believed the police officer's account, a man approached him menacingly and he was frightened. He fired (twelve times), protecting himself by killing his attacker. The people of Ferguson then responded with violence. That's the story a lot of your people heard, America. It is false.

Then there's the other personal version, where Michael Brown approached a white officer, perhaps to speak with him, and the frightened officer killed him, then employed the immunity afforded to police to avoid accountability for an unjustified homicide. In this story, the people of Ferguson were responding to a single unjustified homicide by a police officer in protests which became violent. This story is also false.

The true story is much larger. After the Great Recession, the city of Ferguson, once a mostly white suburb of St. Louis, went through a significant demographic shift, both racially and economically. It became a predominantly Black city and a much poorer city. The city government, however, had not changed to reflect the population, either racially or economically, so a group of much wealthier, whiter people were governing a city that was much poorer and predominantly Black. The government of Ferguson could not sustain its public services in the way it used to, by taxing the property, for a number of reasons. First of all, the Great Recession had diminished the value of all property in the country. Second, white flight meant that the property owners were now white people living outside the city and pressuring the government to lower taxes, while the residents were renters who couldn't pay the taxes through pass-through higher rents. Third, that same white flight meant that property values were driven down by racist attitudes that Black neighborhoods were less valuable, often, ostensibly, because of the false notion that Black neighborhoods are "high crime." But the reason Ferguson, like many Black neighborhoods, became "high crime" was not because of the color of skin of the people who lived there, but because the city decided to fund itself by over-policing its residents. They couldn't support their public services by taxing property, and they couldn't imagine reducing the police budget, so they increased the police budget and made them the de facto IRS for the city, empowering the police to give out more citations to fund city services. The residents of Ferguson found themselves paying for less in the way of parks and libraries and schools and more for police who were supported by a constant barrage of tickets on those people receiving less and less in the way of services for those dollars. And the push for more tickets made the stats swell, producing a city that appeared to have a dramatic increase in crime, thus justifying more spending on the police.

In that context, Officer Wilson accosted Michael Brown. Michael Brown was not a man who was having a single bad interaction with a police officer. He was a resident of Ferguson, a city where almost all the Black people were having nearly constant bad interactions with the police. And one day he turned and started walking back towards that police officer. Maybe he was going to shout at him. Maybe he was going to punch him. Maybe he was going to kill him. We'll never know.

Because Officer Wilson was not a white police officer having a single bad interaction with a Black person he was charged to protect. He was a white officer who made his living from a police force that continually gave out tiny bullshit tickets to fund itself at the behest of a white city council that did not represent that population. He must have felt, on some level, that he was working in a powder keg where someday someone was going to explode. And he saw a man coming at him who was, in some way, going to say, "No." Officer Wilson was a playing card near the top of a very fragile house, and he didn't know if the man coming towards him would attack him or attack the entire, rotten system of Ferguson, Missouri, but either way, the system could not tolerate a person saying, "No." So he defended himself and the rot by murdering Michael Brown.

And when the protesters came out on the streets, they were not just protesting the death of one man. They were protesting a city government that survived by preying upon them. (White) people across the country watched images of residents setting businesses on fire and sneered. "They are just destroying their own town." Precisely. They were lashing out at the very infrastructure of the city that had been attacking them for years.

And you know what you did about it, America? In 2016 you dismissed the last case trying to hold the city accountable. And at a protest on the second anniversary of Michael Brown's murder, someone drove into a group of protesters at a high enough speed to send one of the protesters flying. And you convinced a huge swath of your population that Ferguson was emblematic of the danger Black people posed to white people, fueling the MAGA movement. You passed laws in some places making it legal for people to run their cars into protesters.

And almost no one talks about the role wealth inequality played in the murder of Michael Brown.

Corporate Personhood As Stimulant

It's hard to overstate the negative effects of the Supreme Court's Citizens United decision. Predictably, it didn't immediately destroy democracy. And equally predictably, its pernicious effects have grown over time. If people properly understood the nature of corporations (as I'm sure the justices did), they would immediately have been appalled by the ruling, but lots of people go to work for corporations every day, and everyone interacts with them many times a day, without ever understanding what they are.

A corporation is not just a business like your local

mom-and-pop gas station. By its nature, a corporation is an entity which is an investment vehicle. Sure, it produces cars or cell phones or services like hotel stays or medical insurance coverage, but that's surprisingly ancillary to its main task. If the couple who owns your local mom-and-pop gas station stopped selling gas and started serving breakfast, we would all see this as a distinct business. Not so with a corporation. If a cell phone company shifted to providing streaming entertainment, and eventually stopped selling phones altogether, it's still the same business, because its primary function is not to provide cell phones or streaming entertainment, but to provide a positive return on investment for its shareholders.

Now, let's say this cell phone company realized it could make more money by selling people some new, as-of-yet legal but highly dangerous drug. Not only can that company shift to selling this new, imaginary mega-unicorn-heroin, but if it chose not to out of a sense of morality, and if a shareholder found out about that choice, the shareholder could sue the company for deciding not to maximize the investment. Corporations (unless they incorporate as Benefit Corporations or "B-Corps") are not allowed to make choices based upon the public good. They must choose to make as much money as possible. And the Supreme Court decided corporations, as legal entities, have just as much right to engage in politics as a human being.

Now consider, what if there were some other entity with a similarly constrained set of imperatives. Imagine if we had an organization that was committed to putting poison in the groundwater. Not only did it desire to do this, but it was legally obligated to do this, and if it did anything else, it faced financial penalties. But every time it poisoned a water supply, it benefitted. It had no concern about the people harmed or killed by the water it poisoned. It wasn't allowed to care. This entity did worry lawmakers might pass legislation that would make it illegal for it to poison people's water. Then the Supreme Court said this entity got to participate in making the laws. What legislation would the entity push for immediately? Of course it would try to guarantee its ability to poison water.

If this example seems hyperbolic, research strip mining and hydraulic fracking. There are corporations that make money by poisoning water, and because they are corporations, they can't stop just because they are worried about the people they may poison. And now they have unfettered access to influence government. The only limit on their ability to spend on elections is the amount of money they get paid for poisoning people, and their resources grow with every poisoning. Do the math. It's a terminal business model. More poisoning, more power, more power to poison.

So add that to the list. Because unless you challenge corporate personhood or create an incentive structure that encourages corporations to consider the public good, these vast, powerful entities will drag you down.

How Bad Does the Wealth Inequality Need to Get?

America, your richest 10% now hold 60% of the your wealth. The bottom 50% of your population holds just 6%.

How bad does it have to get before you decide to address this directly? Because you need to understand, the gap naturally widens unless you take direct, intentional action, and as it widens, it accelerates.

Some Leftists have been circulating the idea that your wealth inequality is worse that the wealth inequality in France right before the Revolution of 1798. That's false, and it's a good example of the way we can believe something that confirms our priors. In France, before the Revolution, the proportion of wealth held by the top 10% of the population was about 90%, and the fraction possessed by the top 1% was as much as 60%. That's a lot worse than your 10%/60% and 1%/30% splits. People want to believe you're in a worse situation because it feels bad, America. Instead, they should be worried about the direction you're headed.

It doesn't take an economist to understand that poor people work for money and rich people make money work for them. If someone is living hand-to-mouth, they don't have extra money to invest. Conversely, a wealthy person can only spend so much on their own daily needs. Even if a billionaire spent a hundred times as much on food and clothes and household of four living at the poverty line, the billionaire would only be spending three million dollars a year. Personally, I can't imagine spending three million dollars a year on food, clothing, and housing. Even a ten million dollar mansion doesn't cost three million annually, so unless that billionaire has a bunch of ten million dollar houses which are real residences and not just investments, the billionaire is living on less than a hundred times what that family of four is living on. And if he was a billionaire at the beginning of the year, at the end he has NINE HUNDRED AND NINETY-SEVEN MILLION beyond his (vast) expenses that he has to do something with.

Let's give him a name, shall we? Something like Verve or Vigor or Brio or Elan to capture that special (ketamine filled) pep in his step, but just one letter different so it sounds like a name. So what's Vorve going to do with his $970,000,000? Well, let's say Vorve is really stupid and just sticks it all in the stock market in a no-load S&P index fund. This last year was exceptionally good for him, but let's be more conservative and use the 5 year average (most of which is under a Democratic Presidency which is when the markets do better, but still, being conservative), so Vorve only makes 12.64%. Subtract his 3 million dollars in lavish living, and at the end of the year he has $123 million more than he had at the beginning of the year.

So Vorve starts the next year with a billion plus that $123 million, and he still can't figure out a way to spend more than three million a year on himself and still invests lazily, and gets the same rate of return, so by the end of the next year he has $1,262,397,760. In less than four years he will have two billion dollars.

The family of four living at the poverty level ought to have names, too. Let's give them miserable, peasant names because they are so undeserving. Let's call them Jim and Mary and their two kids Mike and Patty. At the end of the year, Jim and Mary and Mike and Patty will all still be living at the poverty level. They were almost a full THOUSAND MILLION dollars poorer than Vorve and lived on a hundred times less, and four years later they are TWO THOUSAND MILLION dollars poorer than Vorve is.

Now, set Vorve's money aside. Imagine if Vorve went to Subway, and the sandwich artists screwed up his footlong order, so they gave Vorve both the one he ordered and the mess-up. Vorve was skeptical he had the appetite to finish one whole footlong at that moment and knew he certainly wouldn't be able to eat the other. And as Vorve was walking to his car, he heard little Mike asking his mom if he could get a sub, and heard Mary say that they couldn't afford to eat out that month, and Vorve looked right a little Mike, smiled, and *threw his second sub sandwich in the trash.*

America, what would you think of Vorve?

Here's the thing, America. Vorve doesn't throw away one sub sandwich. Vorve lives one hundred times better than little Mike, and he denies him TWO-HUNDRED AND TWENTY-ONE MILLION sub sandwiches. He could buy a sub sandwich for half the people in the United States and still live one hundred times better than Jim and Mary's family for the rest of his life.

And America, you thought he was a douchebag when it was one sandwich, but he's your absolute-fucking-hero when he hoards two hundred million of them. When he refused to share one, you thought he was filth, but when he's got them all, you get a little weak in the knees when he shows up, you tack an extra 30 points to his IQ, and you let Vorve walk the halls of Congress telling any Rep who is up for sale just what they will need to do to make him richer. Vorve is Vorve because of inherited wealth and compound interest and greed, but you let him have more influence over public policy than 90% of your population because Mary and Jim and Mike and Patty can't make campaign contributions. It's a system designed to produce ever increasing corruption.

So no, your wealth inequality is not at the levels of pre-Revolutionary France, but unless you decide to do something about it, that is a mathematical inevitability.

But is little Mike going to grow up to be the guy who mans the guillotine, French Revolution-style? *J'en doute*. Because Jim and Mary are teaching little Mike to be a whole lot more scared of socialism than billionaires. Vorve may do everything he can to make sure little Mike stays at the poverty line, but he believes socialism would take God away.

Maybe It's Religion All The Way Down

America, I'm sure you haven't liked hearing about your institutional racism or classism, but now I'm going to say something that is probably going to piss you off more than anything else I've said. Yes, these systems of oppression intersect, and you can't confront one without dealing with the others, but here's my most controversial theory (and I'm an agnostic, so I'm willing to acknowledge I could be wrong about this): Maybe all of these intersecting systems of oppression are baked in to your religion. And I'm not just talking about your religious oppression of other, non-dominant faiths. That's systemic like your classism and sexism and racism, and you certainly need to deal with your anti-Muslim / anti-Jewish / anti-Pagan / anti-everything-but-a-certain-kind-of-Evangelical-Christianity proclivities which lead to things like banning the travel to and from predominantly Muslim countries and supporting fascism in Isreal under the guise of defending Jews while promoting anti-Jewish hatred. But I suspect, if there's anything that ties all your intersecting systems of oppression together, it's not racism, as some would argue, nor classism, as some would argue, nor even religious intolerance of non-Christians, but your promotion of institutional religion itself.

Like most of your people, I've been raised to admire the way you protect your people's freedom to have the religion of their choice and your commitment to keep your governance separate from the dominance of any specific religious institution. I believed, like most of your people, that this was one of your great strengths, America. But like the Apostle Stephen, I doubt. I need to feel the holes in your hands. Because I suspect you've just proven that was never really a strength at all. It was a weakness gilded by the shinier aspects of religion itself. And now we're going to see what religion has really been about all along.

See, I was raised a Christian in America. In addition to learning the tenets of my own faith, I was also taught this near religious reverence for the way America interacted with Christianity. I was led to believe that Alexis de Tocqueville was right when he wrote

Democracy in America in 1835. I thought, as The Heritage Foundation summarizes de Tocaville, "Modern democratic freedom ... developed as a result of Christianity's influence on European civilization, and more particularly as a result of Puritanism's influence on American civilization. This link is not accidental: Political freedom requires an unshakeable moral foundation that only religion can supply. Moreover, religion is necessary not only to democracy's emergence, but also to its preservation. Democracy fosters intellectual and moral habits that can be deadly to freedom: the tyranny of the majority, individualism, materialism, and democratic despotism. American Christianity acts as a corrective to these perilous democratic tendencies."

But this is wrong. Not just a little bit wrong. Inverted. I just couldn't see it, America. You hid it.

After losing my faith, I maintained, and still maintain, my love and respect for so many Christians, so I need to admit I am trying, desperately, to hold on to some notion that their goodness and kindness and decency is a product of their faith. That's my bias. And the evidence just doesn't support it any more. These people I love are not good and decent and kind because of their religious faith. They are good and decent and kind in spite of their religious faith.

As I mentioned, I'm an agnostic. That means I treat all my own beliefs with a measure of skepticism. I know I have been wrong about things in the past. I know I am not perfect now. It follows that some of my current beliefs are incorrect. As Ludwig Wittgenstein wrote in

Philosophical Investigations, "If there were a verb meaning 'to believe falsely,' it would not have any significant first person, present indicative." I cannot express (or even comprehend) what I currently believe which is incorrect.

However, I can identify which of my beliefs I feel to be more likely to be correct. For example, I believe the sky is blue (or at least appears to be the color my eyes and brain identify as blue) with a degree of certainty which is much higher than the potentially accurate but less likely belief that the sky is olive green with a pattern of very evenly sized chartreuse polka dots. Similarly, there may be a god or a dozen gods or a hundred gods, and I do not confidently deny their existence, but I think the notion that there is a single omnipotent, omniscient, sometimes-loving and sometimes-genocidal creator is less likely than the possibility there is no god at all. Furthermore, I don't think any religious institution is particularly concerned with the nature of the god or gods it purports to believe in. I have come to believe religious institutions are the product of an evolutionary process. In short, they produce a set of dogma which are popular in order to survive and thrive.

Was there a Jesus of Nazareth? I find that highly likely. Were there ten or twenty or a hundred other ascetic dudes walking around sharing their beliefs about the nature of the Jewish G-D and the relationship the people of Roman-occupied Palestine should have with that being? Again, highly likely. Why do we know the teachings of Jesus (as much as we know them, heavily filtered as they likely are)? Because Jesus' teachings are *cool*. He said things that were popular.

That sounds crazy to Christians because, when I was a Christian, we were always being told that the ideas of Jesus were in such opposition to the ways of the world that they got Jesus crucified and caused all his followers to be persecuted for all time. Yes, we were sitting in incredibly expensive buildings filled with the most powerful people in our communities, the bankers and police and political leaders, and we were all nodding along to the idea that were this oppressed minority group because we believed unpopular ideas.

But examine Jesus' ideas in a larger context and you will see an evolutionary progression. Religions which preceded Judaism in the Middle-East, in Africa, in Europe, in South and North America, on the Indian subcontinent, and in East Asia, all held that there were many, many gods, and that these gods were often in conflict, occasionally benevolent, occasionally wrathful, and generally capricious and indifferent. These pantheons functioned because they were useful. They explained the human condition of living at the whims of a natural world which could bless a person with a bountiful harvest one year and wipe that harvest out with a drought or a hail storm or a forest fire the next. To our ancestors, the universe behaved like this pantheon.

The innovation of Judaism was monotheism, but even that comes about through an evolutionary process *within the text itself!* The G-d of Judaism does not begin as the only deity but one of many. When Moses confronts the

Pharoah of Egypt, the Pharoah's priests call upon their gods and turn their staffs into snakes. Moses calls upon his god, and his staff turns into a snake which eats their snakes. Those other gods exist and are capable of supernatural acts, but the god of Moses is more powerful. And let's face it; that idea is cool! In a world of competing pantheons, a group of people who worship a single deity who is tougher than all the other deities is appealing.

Over the course of the text, the other gods cease to be able to do things, and they become false gods. The unified Israelites kick a whole bunch of ass as they move out of Egypt and take a really nice piece of property from all the people who believe in the false gods (though the god of the Israelites apparently doesn't have the foresight to take them to a place with oil underneath it which would have served them well a couple thousand years later). And their story continues to be one about unity. Every time they screw up and turn on one another, they fall apart, and whenever they remember to stick together, continue worshiping the One True God, and maintain their sense of identity, they persevere. And that message is cool! People still like it. It holds them together to this day.

But the deity they believe in is an asshole. That's not just my opinion. Ask your local Rabbi. The deity of the Israelites maintains the qualities of all the pantheons of deities which came before except the incest. He is generally indifferent, occasionally wrathful, occasionally benevolent, and is sometimes seemingly in conflict with

Himself. Why would that be? Because His qualities still mirror the lived experience of human beings dealing with a universe they did not understand which gave and took away at a seeming whim.

A handful of centuries later, people's lives are still pretty fragile things, but they are moderating droughts and floods with massive aqueducts, beginning to learn the basics of medicine, and developing empires like the Roman Empire which seems like it will last forever. They're feeling like things are little bit more in control. And along comes this incredibly kind man who says, "Hey, these Roman gods we're all being pressured to worship are fighting all the time, and the Romans have come here and are fighting with us all the time, and we're back to desperately trying to hold onto our identity like we were when the Babylonians were here, and I just want you all to know that G-d loves you and wants you to love one another. Take care of poor people and widows and prisoners, and G-d will be on your side."

And people were like, "You know, I took this dude's advice, and I went by the local jail and gave some bread to the men who were being held by the Romans, and I dropped some coins in the bowl of the widow who begs on the corner, and then I had this warm feeling. That's G-d! Being nice made me feel a lot better than being a douchebag. And giving the bread to the people in the jail pissed off the Romans, but it wasn't a direct act of war so they had to let it slide, and it felt good to stick it to them, too. I think this Jesus guy is on to something."

This is why Christianity spread throughout the Roman

Empire. Sure, the elites didn't like it, but the ideas were popular with the masses. Many historians have pointed out that the early Christians (who did not have fancy buildings or wealthy televangelists) were basically the social safety net of the Roman world. They got together in houses, taught people to read, provided them with free childcare and medical care and food, and were far more supportive of women and people from other oppressed groups than the Romans or the other religions of the day. Also, they not only refused to charge interest, but they freely gave money to the needy. Cool, right?

Imagine you were a fairly normal person living in the Roman Empire. You were a woman, a slave, you had some kids, and your owner and his children could rape and beat you at will. One day someone approaches you and offers to purchase you and your children out of slavery, provide childcare for your children while you work for yourself, and maybe even offers you a gift of money so you could purchase some goats and a little land to take care of yourself. Your owner, hearing about this conversation, says, "Are you seriously considering forsaking Jupiter and Hestia and Apollo and Mars, all the gods who explain and maintain your current circumstances, and converting to a religion where they believe in three gods who are also one god? It's absurd! One thing cannot be three things, and three things cannot be one thing. Every time I ask one of these Christians about this, they tell me it's a mystery, and if I had enough faith, it wouldn't bother me anymore.

Ridiculous! Surely you can't be considering taking up with that lot." Now, be honest: Would you really care about whether the claims about the three-in-one God of the Christians were true? If they motivated the believers to help you escape your life of abuse and exploitation, wouldn't that be the more important fact to you? The Christians were just cooler.

Yes, cool, but not necessarily true. Just functional. When they got big enough, Emperor Constantine saw them as an existential threat to the Empire. Why? First, people who not only refuse to charge interest but freely give money to the needy are a threat to the financial system. Worse, they refused to fight in the army. They were all pacifists. And that idea is very uncool if you are trying to maintain an empire. So Constantine converted and made Christianity the official religion of the empire. And do you know what he did first? He got all the leaders of the church to agree that it was now completely acceptable for Christians to fight on behalf of their newly Christian empire. And you know what he did second? He sent his newly Christian soldiers to slaughter a bunch of Christians who weren't the right kind of Christians.

And here's the sad reality: That was "cool," in the sense of being functional and popular, just as much as Jesus' idea that nobody should lift a sword against anyone else.

Remember back when you were that slave woman a few seconds ago? Well, now you're one of her grandkids. Christians got your grandmother and mother out of slavery, and you're all living pretty hand-to-mouth and deeply concerned about these frequent incursions by groups attacking and burning villages just like yours on the edge of the Empire. And then someone comes along and says, "Constantine converted. You can now join the army, earn more money than you ever dreamed of, and defend your family from the barbarians. Also, that whole prohibition against usury thing? Well, if you pay an indulgence to the Church, you get a little get-into-Heaven-free card that costs less than what you can make on the interest you charge, so you can now make a profit by loaning money while also making sure you get into Heaven." Would you particularly care about the inconsistency between the previous dogma and the current version? Of course not.

Religions don't persist because their ideas are accurate or consistent. They persist because their ideas are empowering to the priest caste and palatable to the masses. If that gets too out-of-whack, you end up with a priest caste that can't hold onto the masses (the Great Reformation) or a new religion takes hold (e.g. Islam sweeping through North Africa and Southern Europe because the Caliphate was militarily superior and offered a much better way of life to most people).

Now, imagine if some other dogma was True with a capital T. Imagine if there was just one god. He looked like a pig (but not a cute one) from the neck up and an octopus (but not a cute one) from the neck down. His name was Kalooogabeepborp. He sent his holy word down to humans via a prophet named Gary who had a foul body odor, a permanent sneer, and chuckled all the time for no reason. Through Gary, Kalooogabeepborp demanded humans worship him with the sound most pleasing to Kalooogabeepborp's non-human ears which happened to be the screech of poorly played violins. And he dictated that people could only have sex once a year for procreation purposes, that all paintings and buildings had to be painted a single color (Pepto pink), and the only right and proper greeting when meeting a fellow believer in the one true god was to give them a purple nurple. Oh, and Gary's Word dictated that the leaders of the religion should be chosen not by their ability to give comfort and aid to their parishioners or by their wisdom when deciding what direction the flock should go, but by their ability to produce the most boogers which would be the only building material allowed to construct Kalooogabeepborp's temples, so the priests just sat around picking their noses as much as possible and wiping their holy offerings on the booger walls to move up the ranks and prove their devotion to Kalooogabeepborp.

Now, I'm not trying to offend anyone. This example is designed to be as absurd as possible. But consider: If this were True, do you honestly believe that truth would be enough to make it the world's most popular religion? The fifth most popular? The thirtieth? And if we can admit a hypothetically true religion could be less popular than even a single other religion, we must acknowledge some now-dead religion *might* have been True but was relegated to the dustbin of history.

Of course, a devout believer of any modern religion

would counter that their religion's continued existence is the evidence it is favored by the true gods. But if that's the case, longevity and/or the proximity to this moment in time becomes the measure of truth rather than the dogma itself.

And now I will really offend some people, America: Your most popular religion isn't significantly less absurd than the belief in Kalooogabeepborp. Most of your people report some measure of commitment to a particular god who made humans and a devil who tempted them to rebel (poor planning). Then He tried to start over by killing almost everyone with a flood, committed multiple genocides to keep some humans devoted to him, and then had his only kid killed (premeditated hundreds of years in advance) to show humans he loved them. Now he has those humans go into a big room once a week and play pretend cannibalism with crackers and grape juice. Trust a science fiction author, America: If aliens landed on your White House lawn tomorrow, and you had to explain your most popular god to them, they would think you were just as insane as the followers of Kalooogabeepborp.

And that insanity is fine. I've witnessed and even experienced the benefits of religious belief and community. There are advantages to a shared moral framework even if the mythology underlying that framework is inconsistent and easily divorced from the morality itself. The relationships provided by religious communities are often the closest and healthiest ones in people's lives. And a sense of extrinsic purpose can guide us when we can't find an intrinsic compass to make decisions or find the motivation to go on.

I am not one of those people I call "evangelical atheists." I don't feel compelled to take religion away from others. I don't believe, with any degree of religious certainty, that the world would be better off without religion. In general, I find the arguments of evangelical atheists uncompelling. They will point to the statistics of the mass slaughters in religious wars as evidence, as though one more murder caused by a religious motivation compared to one less committed by an atheist demagogue proves the moral justification for atheism.

But America, you do have a religion problem. To return to de Tocaville, the benefits of religion are not in the religion's doctrine itself. De Tocaville thought religion would strengthen you not because of some supernatural divine favor but because of side-benefits: He thought the emphasis on equality that came about through your religious freedom would prevent despotism because people who could choose their own religions would be less likely to cross denominational lines to support a dictator. He thought it would prevent crime because, in Europe, he said, "the criminal is an unfortunate who fights to hide his head from the agents of power; the population in some way assists in the struggle. In America, he is an enemy of the human race, and he has humanity as a whole against him."

But the barriers between Catholics, mainline

Protestants, Evangelicals, and even right-leaning Jews and Muslims have not been enough to keep your people from agreeing on a shared despot, nor have your religions shunned criminality. I once heard a former Evangelical pastor point out that American Christendom has flipped the concept of grace. Ostensibly, grace should be offered to non-Christians to welcome them into the faith, while people within a church should be held to a higher standard by their fellow believers, but American Christendom focuses its ire on non-believers and offers grace exclusively to those within the faith who violate its beliefs. In this formulation of American Christendom, the benefits of religion on democracy evaporate, and the drawbacks of religiosity are direct threats to democracy.

I have to recognize that the danger that's most apparent to me comes from my own break with Christianity. It's likely, if I were LGBTQIA+, I would see the direct intolerance and antagonism of the Church as the most significant threat of religiosity. If I were a Person of Color, I would probably be more sensitive to the deep segregation of American Christendom and the clear hierarchy of power and wealth directed into the hands of the white churches. If I were Indigenous, I would probably focus on the way Christianity was blended with European culture and then used as a pretext to attempt to eliminate my cultural heritage from the face of the earth.

My break with Christianity was not based on politics or metaphysics. I was too deeply ensconced within it to even identify the absurdity of the things I believed, and I made every possible excuse for my fellow Christians when it came to the way the institutional church damaged society because, to me, Christianity was more important than society itself. Christianity was my community and the source of hope for the world, so I couldn't reconcile or really even reckon with the possibility that Christianity was at odds with values like justice and equality. I broke with Christianity (and all religions doctrine) on epistemic grounds.

For those of you who have forgotten that term from your Intro to Philosophy class, while metaphysics focuses on what is really real, epistemology focuses on how we know what we know. I sat there, Sunday after Sunday, reading this text that called on me to be humble and acknowledge that this deity we were worshiping was beyond our comprehension ("'For my thoughts are not your thoughts, / neither are your ways my ways,' declares the Lord. 'As the heavens are higher than the earth, / so are my ways higher than your ways / and my thoughts than your thoughts.'" -Isaiah 55:8-9). And yet we were behaving as though we did understand this deity, knew what it wanted us to do, who it wanted us to criticize and who it wanted us to make excuses for, knew that this religion was the right one and not the one being taught in a building down the street. For me, that was the dealbreaker. It wasn't that the things we believed in frequently manifested in harmful ways in our own lives and in the state of our broader society. I couldn't see those things because I was too close. I just couldn't believe in believing in that way. I needed evidence and logic and consistency. Of course, from within a religious framework, this was a failing on my part. I lacked sufficient faith. But once I was outside that framework, the house of cards fell apart very quickly.

America, do you know how to understand how others see your religiosity? It's surprisingly easy and surprisingly difficult. A religious person who wants to understand how ridiculous his faith must appear to anyone outside that faith needs to only consider the way he thinks about other religions. Or, to quote a guy a lot of your people pretend to admire, "Do unto others as you would have them do unto you." I now reflect on the way I thought about other religions, in fact, the way I was explicitly taught to view them, and I'm shocked that I couldn't see my own in the same way.

"Wait, these Norse people believed a cow came out of the ice and then licked at the ice until a giant came out, and then gods came out of the giant's armpit and killed him and made the world out of his body and the sky out of his skull? That's absurd!"

"Wait, these Mormons genuinely believe a guy was given golden plates with the direct Word of God on them, and he simply lost them? That's ridiculous!"

"Wait, these Hindus believe in thousands of gods but also one god but also everything is god so they are polytheistic, pantheistic, and/or monotheistic? That makes no sense! (But of course our three-in-one God makes total sense and is just fine.)"

"Wait, these Scientologists genuinely believe that

aliens came to Earth and dropped nuclear bombs in volcanoes, releasing their immortal spirits who attach to modern humans and make them think non-Scientology things? That's just silly."

"Wait, these Catholics-" (Yes, I was taught explicitly anti-Catholic doctrine by one old lady in our Presbyterian church.) "-actually believe that the Pope, a human being, can contradict what the previous Pope said, yet both are infallible? That doesn't make any sense!"

And yet, I couldn't say, "Wait, since God was angry with Balaam for doing exactly what God told him to do, God stopped speaking to him (even though he had spoken to him just the previous day), and instead sent an angel to stand in his way (again, while Balaam was doing exactly what God had commanded him to do), only God made the angel invisible to Balaam but not to his donkey, and then, when Balaam got mad at his donkey, God made the donkey talk and told Balaam there was an invisible angel in his way. This story makes no sense! God could have spoken to Balaam (as He had the previous day). God could have made the angel visible. God could have just told Balaam to do the thing and then been satisfied when Balaam was doing exactly that thing. This is like five different kinds of bad communication on God's part. What the fuck?"

But, of course, we were not allowed to say, "What the fuck?" in church or anywhere else.

Once a person escapes the bubble of their own religious upbringing, the more subtle and pernicious contradictions become apparent. No one roots their faith in the story of Balaam and his donkey. But the way I was taught about the concept of grace is foundational to the theology of the church I was raised in, and it was only after I left that I could see it for the horrible force it is. At its root, it's a mixture of two things: forgiveness and hierarchy. We are supposed to forgive others because someone higher on the ladder (specifically the dude at the very top) forgave us, and were supposed to forgive because we're supposed to obey those above us on that same ladder (all the way to the top). This sounds fine if it's not examined too critically. It's only once you leave that you can fully comprehend this is a recipe for abuse. It puts the onus on the victim to forgive the abuser, especially if that abuser is higher on the hierarchy and is therefore someone they are supposed to obey. And the victim is obligated to forgive the abused repeatedly. "I tell you, not seven times, but seventy-seven times." - Matthew 18:22. So if a person is neglected, verbally abused, assaulted, or raped by their parent, spouse, or pastor, they have already been indoctrinated to endure the abuse over and over rather than upset the hierarchy because the hierarchy is the source "from whom all blessings flow" and also the source of the command to forgive.

Now, I'm not saying Christianity itself is necessarily systemically abusive. There is a mechanism in the same sermon to attempt to prevent abuses. Jesus, ostensibly the highest authority, lays out a very clear plan to address abuse. "If your brother or sister sins, go and point out their fault, just between the two of you. If they listen to you, you have won them over. But if they will not listen, take one or two others along, so that every matter may be established by the testimony of two or three witnesses. If they still refuse to listen, tell it to the church; and if they refuse to listen even to the church, treat them as you would a pagan or a tax collector." -Matthew 18:15-17. This should be the counterweight to the command to forgive, right? Except in your churches, America, all the focus is on grace for the people inside the churches (no matter what they are doing to one another), and almost never on booting those who sin … unless the sin is against the institution rather than an individual in the congregation. The teachings about grace protect the Church, not the congregants, and the rare focus on accountability also protects the institution and not the congregants or the broader society.

Now, America, you tell me if I'm wrong about this, because I'm going to put a number on it. How many times has a Christian gone to another, privately, and said, "Look, I'm reading this book we all claim to believe in, and it's very clear that we should welcome foreigners, but I see you cheering on a guy who is starting his run for President by calling all Mexicans rapists and murderers, and that's in direct contradiction to our text, so I think you should repent or leave the church." And then coming back with a friend and saying, "I came to you once by myself, but you have not repented, so I brought this other person, and we know you are the pastor, but this MAGA thing has got to stop or you need to go." And then taking it to the whole church until they all agree that a person who is committed to an ideology of hatred and exclusion needs to be kicked out of their church. Here's my guess about how many times this has occurred, America: Zero times.

Sure, I've seen liberals, including liberal Christians, pointing out the inconsistencies between MAGA Christo-fascism and the version of Christianity they presume Christians ought to believe. Thousands of times. And that's just me. I'll bet there have been millions of calls for Christo-fascists to consider the way their political ideology is inconsistent with a certain liberal interpretation of the Bible. But are they paired with Biblical calls for repentance and the threat of excommunication? Never. And they are all pointless because they miss the fact that these Christians (and yes, these Christo-fascists are Christians despite their liberal critics' denials) do. Not. Fucking. Care. Criticisms of their behavior coming from outside their own faith communities (including, maybe especially, from liberal Christians they see as betrayers) are an attack on their rights, their freedom, their very American-ness which is rooted in their ability to say, "I don't believe that."

The mistake too many liberals make (and whoo-boy, I have certainly made this mistake far too many times) is to project our epistemological framework onto those on the right and expect the arguments which would persuade us to persuade others. Rational, scientific thinking dictates that claims should be testable and disprovable. But faith-based claims are bulletproof. To understand why, we need to distinguish between a lie, hypocrisy, and a third thing they call "faith."

If I know 2+2=4 but say 2+2=5 because I want you to believe something I know to be untrue, I am a liar.

If I say I believe 2+2+4 but then behave as though 2+2=3 or 2+2=5 whenever I make change so I can rip you off, I am a liar and a hypocrite.

If I say I believe 2+2=5 and can't be dissuaded by a clear demonstration that a couple apples and another couple apples make four apples, I have a deep and abiding faith that 2+2=5.

And if I say 2+2=5, refuse to acknowledge your apple demonstration, and then tell you 2+2=3 which I do not believe so I can make change as though 2+2=3 and 2+2=5 whenever it is convenient for me to rip you off, I am a liar, a hypocrite, and a person immune to argument because of my faith.

We need a term for this. Some have proposed the term "post-truth," as though this is a phenomenon that has come about at a specific point in time after people lived in some agreement about the truth. Some have called it "willful ignorance," and while this captured the fact that it's a combination of intent and behavior and lack of knowledge, I think "willful ignorance" is better applied to smaller, individual instances than an ideological framework that motivates behaviors in many spheres of a person's life. I propose we call people who are all three "full of shit" to acknowledge we have always had some of these people living in our midst, and to capture the way this combination of deceit, hypocrisy, and faith, when deeply rooted, fill a person up with something that is malicious (lies), repugnant (hypocrisy), and ubiquitous (faith).

And yes, we all lie.

And yes, we all are hypocrites.

And yes, we are all people of faith. Even the most skeptical, scientific minds believe things they cannot prove and act on those beliefs every single day.

But being full of shit is different. This isn't telling someone they look good in those jeans because you've decided they need a pick-me-up more than an accurate assessment. That's an isolated, little lie. This isn't saying people should try to eat more healthily and then grabbing a cookie when no one is looking. That's an instance of hypocrisy. And this isn't presuming the sun will rise tomorrow without any more ontological proof than the somewhat paltry evidence that it always has in the past. That's faith.

Being full of shit is dangerous. It's harmful to the person who is full of shit, and it's harmful to others. When faith and hypocrisy and lying are mixed and deeply rooted, a person is easily manipulated and is willing to participate in manipulating others. Because lying is an essential component, being full of shit is contagious; the person who is full of shit believes things that are false, acts in ways that are inconsistent with their own beliefs, and tries to make others believe the things they believe.

Like I said, it's bulletproof. This recipe is immune from demonstrations of falsehood because of the shield of faith, immune from accusations of hypocrisy because of the willingness to lie, and immune to appeals to truth because of hypocrisy. The elements protect one another.

And it's testable. Instead of demonstrating a lie or pointing out hypocrisy and saying, "Gotcha!" ask a person what it would take for them to be persuaded they are wrong. As they contemplate the answer, if you are like me, you will have to bite your tongue, because your impulse will be to provide examples. Resist. A person who is persuadable will be able to think of things that would change their mind. A person who is full of shit will not. They will lash out at you instead. Because they are not interested in truth. They are interested in protecting themselves from the enemy of their faith.

Josh Dawes, the host of the *The Great Awokening Podcast* where he claims to help Christians "deconstruct wokeness," tweeted this advice to his followers: "It's okay to use deception in service of defeating the left. It's not sinning in order to do good. It's being righteously shrewd in order to do good. It's also okay to enjoy it. Lighten up."

Aldous Huxley could have been writing about this very inversion of Christian morality when he wrote, "To be able to destroy with good conscience, to be able to behave badly and call your bad behavior 'righteous indignation' — this is the height of psychological luxury, the most delicious of moral treats."

You see, America, the problem is not metaphysical or even moral but epistemological. As long as a vast amount of your populace says, "Everyone else's beliefs are stupid, but mine are right regardless of the inconsistency or the evidence to the contrary, and I should lie to protect my beliefs, and I get to enjoy the harm I cause because it's against the unrighteous," you're going to have a very hard time making public policy decisions that have any basis in reality, but you will make public policy that is designed to harm people.

Let's say, purely hypothetically, that there is a deadly plague, and the only way to stop it is to have people take medicine not just for their own benefit, but to prevent the spread of the plague to others. If you are filled with people who say, "I don't care what anyone else says. It's against my religion to take the medicine," you cannot appeal to their sense of concern for their fellow citizens because that's irrelevant to them, or at least it is superseded by their faith, and they'll see your efforts to preserve the lives of your citizens as a direct attack on that faith.

Or let's say, again, hypothetically, that your people are releasing poison which is building up over time and will eventually make the world uninhabitable for their great-grandchildren. But those people say to you, "Sorry, America, but I just don't believe in that danger. That's my religion." What can you do about that, America? Nothing. Unless you address the epistemological problem of permitting faith as a justification for any behavior, you're fucked. And so is every other animal and plant that likes to live at a temperature less than 150°.

And America, if you'll permit me just one more

hypothetical, I think your religion problem will become clear. Let's say, purely hypothetically, that a leader rose to prominence who violated all Ten Commandments and Jesus' two big Greatest Commandments frequently and publicly. And let's say a majority of your self-proclaimed Christians sang hymns to him and made golden statues of him and in every other conceivable way made an idol of this false god. When those people claimed they believed in those commandments, any reasonable person would say they were full of shit. But you, America, give them a special dispensation to make public policy because you are protecting their religious freedom, their freedom to be full of shit.

To get very non-hypothetical, one of my neighbors was a retired corrections officer. He spent an entire career maintaining the punishments you dictate for violating your laws by keeping felons separated from the general public. I'm willing to bet all my money he never once said, "This felon here seems nice. I'll just let him leave the prison today. And then maybe I'll vote for him to be our town dog catcher. He would do a fine job with my tax money." But this neighbor of mine hung a Trump flag in front of his house. Now, how can a person who spends his whole working, adult life enforcing the idea that felons deserve to be in prison suddenly fly a flag supporting putting a felon in the White House? Simple. He refuses to believe Donald Trump is really a felon, and that everyone who is not on his team is so dangerous that this not-a-felon should be President. There is no amount of evidence that can sway him. Why not?

Because he's full of shit.

More broadly, how can Christians decide they need to do everything they can to harm Trans people under the pretext of protecting women in bathrooms and women athletes, then turn around and support a man who has been credibly accused of rape by more than 20 victims, found criminally liable of sexual assault in court, bragged about committing sexual assault on tape, and has even been credibly accused, under oath, of raping a 12 year-old girl and a 13 year-old boy? Easy. They simply do not believe he did any of those things (including the things he, himself, said he did on tape). They don't believe Trump is a rapist (faith), they don't really care about harm to women (hypocrisy) and they say they care anyway (lies) because they are full of shit.

And, lest any liberal Christian try to hide from their part in this, America, how many of your liberal Christians can honestly say they worship Jesus and try to keep his commandments if they haven't ever gone to one of their MAGA-idolizing brethren and told them to repent or leave the church? Blue State Christians need to sit with that. Their Lord and Savior told them the exact procedure to expel unrepentant sinners from their midst, and none of them have done it because... Because it's just politics? Because it would be uncomfortable? Because they know they are not in the majority in their churches? I'm not a Biblical scholar, but I don't see any caveats in Jesus' teachings about politics or discomfort or being in the majority. I have listened as some of the most faithful, devout Christians I know have leaned towards me and whispered, "This guy we've invited to sit at our table is a Trumper, so don't talk politics around him." No, America, your Christianity is a problem because your conservative Christians are full of shit and your liberal Christians are *also* full of shit. These liberal Christians say they believe in Jesus' teachings (faith), don't really want to kick anyone out of their churches (hypocrisy), and tell themselves they are the ones who really care about what Jesus said (lies), because they are full of shit.

You have made religion an excuse to reject any inconvenient truth, and you have elevated the religion which promotes behavior most antithetical to its own doctrine. I don't see how you can ever deal with your other pressing, systemic problems as long as "I refuse to believe that because I'm full of shit" is legitimate American political discourse.

So how should a person who is not full of shit respond when they find that a person is unpersuadable and their beliefs are harmful? Simple: Leave. Close the social media app, walk away from the conversation, get up from the table, deny the contagion the ability to spread to you. The person who is full of shit is not evil or even consciously malicious (though spreading falsehoods knowingly is malicious). They are acting out of a sense that they are protecting themselves and their group. They are doing what they think is best. The only way they will unwind the knot of lies and hypocrisy and faith-based truth claims is to decide they want to and go to work on that knot themselves. If being full of shit becomes completely socially unacceptable, maybe more of them will take a hard look at the shit they are filled with, but no one else can make that happen. And no one can make it happen for you, America, once the contagion of full-of-shit-ness is your majority. Society cannot deny itself society. This is you, now, unless you decide you don't want it to be. And a person who wants to avoid accepting a full-of-shit ideology which becomes the dominant culture can best do so by leaving that culture, in whatever shape that leaving needs to take.

"I'm getting too old for this shit."

Up until our breakup, I taught 14-18 year-olds for 24 years. Let me tell you, America, nothing will make you feel old like hanging out with 14 year-olds all day. I know age is relative, but, during my career, the relatives shifted from "Oh, you're a young teacher. You're younger than my older brother," to "You're not that old, Mr. Gorman. You're still younger than my dad," to "Mr. Gorman, you taught my dad."

And that's to say nothing of the slang. I taught through "bomb" and "swag" right up to "skibidi." I am old enough to remember Danny Glover's Roger Murtaugh repeatedly saying "I'm getting too old for this shit," and laughing at that old man, and now I am six years older than Danny Glover was when he said that line. I am too old for this shit.

In my lifetime, I've watched as an aspiring candidate for the presidency had to drop out of the race in disgrace when photos were leaked of him hanging out with a model friend. Gary Hart is 88 now, and he has got to be so pissed. Then I watched as revelations of Bill Clinton's extramarital affair bogged down his presidency. I didn't know about the rape allegations, nor did I know that the person leading the charge to oust him, Newt Gingrich, had cheated on multiple wives and had even traded in one wife for a younger one while his wife was dying of cancer. But I did know the Republican party considered itself the "Party of Family Values" and the "Defenders of Traditional Marriage" at the time. I watched as another Democratic hopeful had the courage to openly talk about class stratification and the "Two Americas," only to have his political ambitions undone by his extramarital affair, also while his wife was dying of cancer. I wonder if John Edwards seethes when he sees that Newt Gingrich is still making the rounds as a talking head on right-wing media.

And now we are about to have a President who not only cheats on his multiple wives, but sexually assaults women and children. Now, I'm not some Puritan who thinks the only measure of a person's legacy is their marital fidelity. When Clinton was embroiled in the repercussions of the Lewinsky affair, his contemporary in France, Jacques René Chirac, was revealed to have engaged in multiple affairs, and the French people essentially collectively shrugged. A person could still be a competent leader and a bad spouse, though it does call their judgement into question. That's not my point, though. What strikes me is the trajectory.

Like most middle-class, white, liberal boys, I was raised to believe in this notion of inevitable progress. I was taught a superficial version of both world and American history which said that things always went from worse to better. The Revolutionary War freed Americans of the Monarchy and gave white, land-holding men the right to vote. The good guys then fought against the bad guys to free the slaves and give Black men the right to vote. Then the good guys gave women the right to vote. Then they stopped making kids work in mines, and then they started giving old people Social Security checks. Then some brave Black people walked across a bridge and held a huge rally at the mall in DC, and that ended Segregation and really gave Black people the right to vote. (Note: Not a single mention of Latino people or Asian people or Indigenous people or LGBTQIA+ people anywhere in the history I was taught.) And then our biggest problem was a President getting a blowjob, and we beat the USSR forever and invented the Internet and some crazy religious zealots smashed planes into skyscrapers so we unified the world, and then we ended racism by electing a Black President. The end.

In my insulated, privileged bubble, it seemed natural

to believe that when Martin Luther King Jr. (I was taught a version of King who was just a very nice man who never challenged the status quo except when it came to Segregation, of course) said the moral arc of history was long but bends towards justice, this described the natural progression towards the kind of egalitarianism I'd been led to believe I lived in. And if Steve and Tom could just get married and adopt 2.5 kids and live a "normal" life in their house with the white picket fence, everything would be wrapped up with a bow. Roe would never be overturned because even the Republicans knew they would be the dog who caught the mail truck, and we were just a few decades away from faster-than-light travel and Klingons and Vulcans hanging out with us in harmony as we adventured on Star Trek: The Next Generation.

I had never personally experienced a backlash of any kind. I was living through the Third Wave of feminism, going to college in Washington State, listening to alternative music from Seattle without knowing about the Riot Grrl scene just down in Olympia, and I was watching Joe Biden chair the Senate Judiciary committee and decide to only allow Anita Hill to testify (so it wouldn't turn into a "circus"), and it seemed like a he-said-she-said situation to me. I didn't understand what "waves" even meant.

America, I wonder if you are as naïve as I was. Maybe, because most of you is composed of people who have experienced backlashes, you understand this on a deeper level than I do. Or maybe, in spite of real, lived experience, most of you have bought into the same myth I was taught. But the moral arc of history does not bend towards justice, America. It must be bent through hard work, and it snaps back when pushed. As Octavia Butler wrote, ignorance is not passive.

> "Beware:
> Ignorance
> Protects itself.
> Ignorance
> Promotes suspicion.
> Suspicion
> Engenders fear.
> Fear quails,
> Irrational and blind,
> Or fear looms,
> Defiant and closed.
> Blind, closed,
> Suspicious, afraid,
> Ignorance
> Protects itself,
> And protected,
> Ignorance grows."

You have not faced a great leap backwards since Reconstruction, a period of American history that was entirely eliminated in my K-12, undergrad, and master's degree education. Do you even remember it, America, or have you successfully protected your ignorance? The moral arc of history can bend towards injustice. It has all over the world, and it has right here in the United States. Ask the women of Iran if things always move towards progress. Ask the people of Russia if the fall of one kind of despotism leads to a flourishing of democracy. And look within yourself to see if a cataclysmic civil war and the emancipation of slaves necessarily leads to equal justice and fair representation.

A civilization can go backwards. You have before, and you are doing it again. You don't want to believe me, America, but let me offer you the best example I can: The canary in the coal mine is a mockingbird.

It's Not a How-To Book

It's tricky to calculate exactly because schedules change and sometimes a school year will be interrupted by a global pandemic, so some years I taught it more than others, but over the course of my teaching career I believe I've taught the novel *To Kill a Mockingbird* 95 times. I probably wouldn't have ever cracked that 100 mark because I've been advocating that we move away from the novel since it's written from a distinctly white perspective and targeted at a white audience. There are newer, higher-interest novels which illustrate the same points in ways that connect better with my modern, majority-minority students. But it is a great book, and everyone should read it at some point in their lives. You might not remember the Reconstruction Era, America, but I'm guessing the vast majority of your people have been exposed to this novel or the movie at some point. That was the argument for keeping it in the curriculum; a shared cultural narrative. I do want my students to be able to go out into the world and at least get the references.

Teaching *Mockingbird* is demanding for a lot of reasons. The vocabulary level is difficult for my students, especially those learning English as a second or third language. The perspective from which the story is told is unusual. It's not told from a child's perspective like the middle-grade books my students have read before they come to me, nor from a teenage perspective like most of the YA titles they consume, nor from an adult's perspective exactly. It's told by an adult Jean Louise Finch reflecting on the time when she was six and seven and went by Scout. Consequently, I'm asking 14 and 15 year-olds to simultaneously empathize with a six year-old and a thirty-something (presuming the narrator is about the same age as Harper Lee was when she wrote the book). Those cognitive tasks are difficult enough to be barriers for some young (and some not-so-young) readers. But the bigger challenges are historical and sociological context.

It takes weeks to prepare students to read *Mockingbird* because the book is set during the Great Depression, but it was published in 1960 and was telling white Northerners about Segregation. The book's popularity (and the success of the film that came out very quickly after, in 1962) were important elements of waking up white people and accelerating the Civil Rights movement. But my students come into my class knowing almost nothing about either time period.

Here in Oregon, we teach a lot about the Oregon Trail. Then, in order to contextualize the reading of excerpts from *The Diary of Anne Frank*, we teach students about The Holocaust. They get broad overviews of other bits of history, but basically they come into my class having learned some people on the East Coast made a heroic journey to Oregon, and then, far away in Europe, Germans were really awful to Jews, then the USA saved the day, and then later they were locked in their rooms by Covid. Everything in between is blurry at best, and they have no real concept of when the Oregon Trail occurred except that it was before World War II which was before Covid.

So I would spend a lot of time trying to explain The Great Depression, Segregation, and the Civil Rights movement, then lecturing on the concept and history of race, the four waves of feminism, and different concepts of gender and sexuality (Lee's Scout is arguably Trans and/or Asexual, but Lee and her readers wouldn't have had language for those concepts, though they did exist in medical literature, and students need to be able to identify and analyze Lee's critiques of gender norms). I would teach about socio-economic class distinctions as they manifested in the American South during Segregation, and anything else I could think of that my students needed in order to critically read Harper Lee's *To Kill a Mockingbird* and discuss it with their peers using a shared vocabulary.

And here's the thing, America: The essential concepts I taught over the course of my career didn't change much, year after year. Yes, I too was learning, so my own vocabulary and conceptual framework were evolving, and some of the language about concepts like race and gender were also changing over that time period, but aside from some new verbiage, the pre-reading didn't change very much. Do you know what changed, America? You did.

At the beginning of my career, the idea that a Black man shouldn't be convicted in a sham trial and then executed by law enforcement was uncontroversial. By the end, it was "woke." Ultimately, to protect myself and the school from the telephone game of students telling parents some variation of what I'd said, and then those parents filtering it through a Fox News-fueled fever dream before storming into the administration, I had to film my lecture on race and racism. That way any angry parent would have to point to what angered them specifically, and if my employers had chosen to censor me or retaliate in any way (which they did not do), the district would have had to support those specific critiques. None of these complaints resulted in disciplinary action, but the complaints did increase in frequency and fervor as the years went on.

America, one common mistake my student would make was to accidentally refer to *To Kill a Mockingbird* as "How To Kill a Mockingbird," and I would make a big show of getting mock-exasperated and shout, "It's not a how-to book!" But in order to understand the central tragedy of this novel, one must first understand that Black lives matter. But the notion that the lives of Black people have intrinsic worth has become controversial, and once a large percentage of my students felt accepting that would be a betrayal of their political ideology, they simply closed themselves off to the book entirely. Some would say, directly, "This isn't what my family believes." Others would storm out to head to the office to call home or report me to the administration. A lot of them just zoned out (and not in the way some students always zone out. I taught for 24 years. I know the difference between bored indifference and active, rigid rejection of uncomfortable content). But they couldn't ever clearly articulate their opposition. Because the only other way to understand the book is as a blueprint to repeat it. Either the book is about the truism that it is a sin to kill a mockingbird, or the novel is about how to kill a mockingbird and get away with it.

You have not yet reached the point where you were prohibiting me from teaching *To Kill a Mockingbird* (at least not in Oregon) or forcing me to teach it as a lesson in how to recreate Segregation, but America, I'm telling you, your culture is shifting in that direction. Your next generation will not save you if they are already being indoctrinated into that white supremacist, Christo-fascist ideology that dictates any teaching about class, gender, or racial justice is "woke" and a threat to their tribal identity.

In my lifetime, America, your culture has shifted in such a way that white people have gone from refusing to talk about racism, to saying, "I'm not a racist," to "You may call me a racist for saying this, but..." to "I'm proudly anti-woke." You've gone from a broadly accepted belief that women at least ought to have equal rights and opportunities to "I'm not a feminist," to prominent conservative pundits publicly saying, "It was a mistake to give women the right to vote." You've gone from an arch-conservative president quoting John Winthrop's notion of "a shining beacon on a hill" and saying "and the doors were open to anyone with the will and the heart to get here," to a president calling immigrants "vermin" and other countries "shitholes." The moral arc of your history is not bending towards justice, America.

Only a few years ago, there was a lively debate amongst liberal activists and pundits about whether or not this new honesty was helpful. After all, the thinking went, since the material conditions, the public policies, and the underlying systems were not significantly better or worse for many oppressed groups than they had been only a few years before, perhaps this new honesty would facilitate more open dialogue about those conditions, policies, and systems now that people weren't hiding behind "I'm not a racist," and "Women ought to have equal rights," and "The doors are open." Now that the rhetoric of the oppressors was more closely aligning with the lived experience of the oppressed, maybe the masses could see the systems for what they were.

The other side of that argument said this flourishing of openly racist, misogynistic, and xenophobic rhetoric would fuel more hatred rather than reveal systemic injustice. I didn't weigh in on this debate because it was mostly being carried out by marginalized people, and I didn't feel it was my place to share my opinions, but I found both sides very persuasive at the time. I remember one of my favorite pundits making the case that while the right was winning the PR war, the left was winning in every sphere of social and political life, so the right could be dismissed as merely angry reactionaries responding to the left's clear dominance in elections and in boardrooms and in households and on the streets. Everyone, it seemed, was trying to be more inclusive and forward-thinking, and even the right was looking for more women and people of color to be their mouthpieces as they groused about diversity. Who cared if rightwing AM radio was a cesspool of bile? It was strategically useful to have people self-identify, right?

Wrong.

One of my favorite authors is Octavia Butler, and I love the origin story of her novel *Kindred*. As I understand it, this is how that book came to be: Butler, though never given the respect she was due, did become a prominent enough figure in the world of science fiction literature to be asked to appear on panels at science fiction conventions. There she would sit alongside almost exclusively white, male colleagues talking about a white, male dominated genre of literature and fielding audience questions. Frequently, as people asked about ideas that are popular in science fiction, someone would ask the panelists about time travel. Oblivious to Butler's identity and presence, the white men would talk about how great it would be to travel back to romanticized times of white, male heroism, like medieval Europe or the American Civil War, and Butler would have to explain, over and over, that time travel stories, at least back into the past, held no appeal for her because there was no time in history that would have been better for her as a Black woman. Eventually she got so tired of explaining why she didn't want to write that kind of book that she decided she had to write that kind of book to show them what she was talking about. And that's how we got *Kindred*, a brilliant novel about a Black woman who is sucked back in time to the antebellum South and immediately enslaved and tortured.

In 1979, Octavia Butler could honestly say life was better for a Black woman than it had ever been before in history, and I'll bet, if she'd been asked in 1993, when she wrote *Parable of the Sower*, and again in 1997 when she wrote *Parable of the Talents*, she would have said life for a Black woman in America had significantly improved since 1979. But read those books, America. Octavia Butler knew the progress she'd experienced in her life was not an inevitability, and that things could get worse, at first slowly, and then very quickly.

And here's a scary truth you need to sit with, America: If a modern gay, Black, female science fiction author were offered a working time machine or a panel attendee's hypothetical one, she might reasonably choose to go back to the time before Roe was overturned, or right after the Obergfell decision but before the current backlash, or after Me Too but before Gamergate. America, this is not the best time in your history. That may still be yet-to-come, but that's not an inevitability. And here's my very scary prediction: If you asked that same author the same question in two or three years, she might say she would like to go back to the late summer of 2024. And the white, straight, male science fiction author sitting next to her will agree. Because I suspect it's going to get so much worse that you, America, all of you, will agree the past was better.

That shared realization will not save you because fascism is inherently regressive and intentionally harmful. It's a doom spiral that will make everyone wish they could Make America Great Again. The (very intentional) way to unite everyone around the MAGA flag is to make life in the United States maximally miserable for as many people as possible. All the political incentives now align around that objective for everyone on both sides of the political spectrum. Republicans want life to get worse to keep their base angry, and now Democrats want life to get worse to prove Trump can't govern, but also that they aren't too extremely different from the winning side. Think about that, America. Your dominant ideology is a clear plan explaining how to kill all the mockingbirds.

Can I Have My Favorite T-Shirt Back?

And now we come to that particularly awkward part of a breakup where I have to ask you for some things, America. In this part of a breakup, one or both parties have to make a focused appeal and intentionally ignore so much about their former partner.

We have to look beyond their physical body we were once (and maybe still are) attracted to. Do not ask for a last kiss or a last role in the hay. It's at-best unsatisfying and at-worst humiliating.

We have to look beyond the mind we once connected with. At this point in a breakup, the other person has just been hit with a barrage of uncomfortable realizations and can't be expected to make the kind of insightful comments or witty jokes we once found so endearing. They get to be a blubbering mess or a silent statue if they need to be.

We even have to look beyond the heart we once depended upon for love and comfort and concern. The other person is likely wondering if they ever loved us, why they ever loved us, and if that love was a mistake. It's no time to appeal to their feelings.

Instead, we have to make a direct appeal to their conscience. Either one party or both have now made the choice to transition away from being a good partner, but we can at least hope everyone wants to be a good ex moving forward. That's the part of our former partner we're looking at when we say, "Can I have my favorite T-shirt back?"

Thus, even though this letter is to you, America, for this last bit I'm ignoring your body politic. That part of you have made themselves fully known to me. They were offered an ideology of hatred, and a majority of them either got up off their couches and voted for it or sat on their couches and didn't vote against it. If pressed, the vast majority of that majority would say the hatred wasn't what got them off the couch or kept them on it. They would say, though they don't fully understand tariffs or inflation, that they have a vague sense that the ideology of hatred might make them a little bit richer. In other words, they are willing to tolerate the hatred out of a combination of ignorance and selfishness. To put it bluntly, America, I am not making an appeal to your body politic because I find your body completely unappealing. Ew.

And I'm not appealing to your mind. From where I sit, your smartest people are using their intellects to actively justify their passivity and silence. They are the most aware of your history, of the phenomenological possibility of rapid social decline, and of the fragility of systems, and all this knowledge compelled them to be quiet, anxious wrecks for the last six months. I'm not counting on your mind being much help, America.

I'm also not appealing to your heart. While your right ventricle is passionate about their hatred, your left ventricle, those loudest, most passionate Leftist voices, have revealed themselves to be dangerously useless. I used to think the people on the far left were valuable because they shifted the Overton window, helping people like me who were more moderate consider new ideas that would someday become public policy. But America, your left ventricle is full of grifters who are either shouting about anticapitalism in the hopes of cashing in on increased follower counts, or those posturing more privately for their black-bloc buddies by sneering and laughing about how they wouldn't be caught dead at something as centrist as the Women's March. As has frequently been pointed out, the far left and far right are a horseshoe, the most extreme willing to flip for cash or prizes. With the possible exception of Luigi Mangioni, none of these people seem to have much interest in doing anything anymore. When they had the chance to do something real, they chose not to. Anyone who spends more energy mocking moderates than trying to move them isn't serious. America, your Leftists should be taken exactly as seriously as the tangible change they attempt to produce, which is to say not very seriously at all. So no, I am not appealing to your heart, America.

Instead, I'm asking a small bit of you, your Jiminy Cricket, for some last favors as we finish this breakup. The kind of blue-state or blue-dot-in-a-red-state left-leaning pragmatist who would read a letter like this all the way to the end is the only conscience you have left, and I know I've upset even that sliver of you in these pages by poking at their inaction and denial and faithless faithfulness. But if this little part of you wants to be a good ex, America, here are the favors I'm asking for:

1.   Be Rude

You've tried being civil. What has that accomplished? When you bit your tongue as your uncle talked about how Mexicans were ruining the country, did your silence help any Mexican Americans? It certainly helped your uncle. It made the xenophobia sound like acceptable dinner table conversation to your cousins who were nodding along. You traded a welcoming nation for a slightly less uncomfortable Thanksgiving dinner. Fuck that. Be the annoying person. The one no one wants to invite to Thanksgiving because you make them feel bad about their own silence. Be that person until everyone in the family would rather be as annoying as you are than be your racist uncle. I once heard a bartender I deeply respect say that when a Nazi comes into your bar, you kick him out right away, or else you are now working at the Nazi bar. Stop trying to be nice to the wrong people. It's alright to be rude.

2. Try Not to Fund Fascism

This will be impossible. Let's accept that right away. If you are an adult living in a society, you will contribute to the outcomes of the society you inhabit. When I went around knocking on doors for Barack Obama, I became responsible for every drone strike against every hospital he bombed. And I did it again, knowing that, because I knew there would be a lot less murder (and rape and pillaging) from those murderous drone strikes than from the boots-on-the-ground invasions the other guy was promising. The people telling you not to accept the lesser of two evils are ignorant and irresponsible. You support evils every single day when you pay your bills and go to your job and generally engage in adulting. Refusing to vote while you pay your taxes isn't righteous, it's stupid. You will support even what you didn't vote for anyway, so try to make your vote count for a little less evil the next time you're paying your taxes.

But here's a little secret. Do you know what will probably happen to you if you forget to pay your taxes at the end of the year? Nothing. And the next year? Probably also nothing. And if the Trump administration and the Republicans in your state legislature have their way when it comes to defunding the IRS, do you know what becomes even more likely when you don't pay your taxes? Even more nothing. And if they do catch up with you, you pay the taxes and a little fine. A tax on your unwillingness to pay taxes. Now, I'm not sure the First Amendment extends to telling people not to pay their taxes, so I am absolutely not saying that. I'm saying you should seriously consider giving Donald Trump's government just as much as he's shown you he's given to that government when his taxes have come due. I'm a big fan of a lot of the things taxes pay for. I like libraries and fire departments and public schools and Medicare and Medicaid and food stamps. I don't want those to be defunded. But spend some time thinking about where your line in the sand is located, and when they start building the camps in the desert, consider not paying for them.

You can also stop giving so much to the individuals and companies that support fascism. One of the big pushes under any fascist regime is privatization. The demonstrably false pretext is that the private sector is inherently more efficient than the public sector, so providing government services via private companies will save money. This almost never works in practice. Why? Because a private company is actually at a disadvantage when it comes to providing lower-cost services. Private companies have to make a profit, so that cost is tacked on to everything they do. Even if they can find enough efficiencies to cut costs below the cost of public servants plus profit (mostly by underpaying their workforce), their management class demands much higher pay than public sector management. So keep an eye out for the companies who are angling to do more business with the Trump administration. As much as you can, avoid supporting them.

Again, you're not going to be able to avoid supporting grocery store conglomerates or gas companies, but you can try. Ignore those people who tell you boycotts don't make a difference. They're just wrong. Boycotts make a huge difference even if they don't immediately affect the bottom line of the company you're avoiding. They make a difference because they change *you*. It's like recycling. Recycling doesn't do much of anything for the planet. In fact, unbeknownst to you, you may be separating your garbage into two bins only to have your local sanitation service put them all back together in a single landfill. That happened in my town for a while, and they didn't announce it, nor did they announce an end to the practice, so for all I know they may still be putting the recycling in the local dump. But that's not really why recycling matters. Recycling makes a huge difference because it changes people's behavior in other areas of their lives. People who bother to recycle start to see themselves as people who care enough to about the environment to go to the trouble, and that has a measurable affect on their voting patterns and other consumption habits. The recycling is a kind of ritual, and the repetition of the ritual changes the person. So find some businesses to boycott. Even though you are still going to fund the actions of the MAGA right in a host of different ways, the exercise of trying not to will remind you not to completely capitulate.

3.   If You Can't Be Loud, Support Those Who Can

Everyone does not have the equal ability to voice their opposition to the regime that's coming to power. Be honest with yourself about your limits. Could you have done more to prevent this? Almost certainly. Did you avoid it because it would have been deadly, dangerous to you or your family, uncomfortable, or just mildly inconvenient? If things get worse, as I expect they will, the very same action that would have been mildly inconvenient will become uncomfortable, and the same thing that would have been uncomfortable will become dangerous and maybe even deadly.

So look around for the people who are doing what

you cannot. And then find out how to support them. The best way is to find out how to support them is to ask them directly. Some people will need moral support. Others financial. It will vary. But ask, and you'll be surprised by how easy it is.

When I think of the people I want to support, my bias goes immediately to artists and authors because I'm in their community. You may think of other people who push back from other angles. But I want to describe some ways to support artists and authors because I think it illustrates just how surprisingly easy it is to lift up the people who are doing what you can't.

Jiminy Cricket America, let's say you come across a piece of artwork on social media that directly challenges the rightward movement of America more broadly. The smallest thing you can do is give it a "like" or whatever the equivalent of that is on your platform of choice. It seems like a tiny thing because it is, but tiny things add up, and if lots of Jiminy Cricket Americans take that same tiny action you just did, it's amplified by the algorithm, and now lots more people, including those outside Jiminy Cricket America, will see that piece of artwork and know not everyone is on board with the regime. And that may give someone else the courage to push back in some other tiny way. It all makes a difference.

But suppose you feel safe enough to do a little more for that artist than just give her post a "like." Follow her account and like all her other work. So far this has cost you zero dollars and maybe ten pleasant minutes of your time.

Want to do a little more? She probably has a print for sale. If you can afford it, buy it. Then, when it arrives at your house, if you can afford it, put it in a frame. Even if you can't afford a frame, hang it up on the wall. Then take a picture of it on your wall and post that image on the artists page. Even better, post it on your own page and tag the artist. Now you have given her money, publicity, and moral support. And even if you are exceptionally slow with your phone camera and typing and posting, this will have cost you about twenty dollars and twenty minutes of your time, and you get to live in a place with that moving piece of artwork on your wall.

I've done this maybe a dozen times. I wish I'd done it more, even though I had to take those works out of their frames and box them up to move them to the other side of the world. And you know what I'll do with them there? Buy new frames and hang them up and take pictures and post them. Because it matters. And it's cheap and easy.

What about writers who are crafting the books and short stories and articles and blog posts that say the things you cannot say, or who are saying them in the way you wish you could have said them to your uncle at Thanksgiving? Again, it's shockingly easy. When I'm commiserating with my fellow authors, we often laugh sadly about the lack of support we receive for our work. It's not the money (though it's certainly that, also), but the incredibly low threshold for moral support which would make a huge difference. I frequently point out that I have friends who would drop everything and spend an entire Saturday hauling boxes if I asked them to help me move, but if I asked them to rate and review a book (not even to read it, just rate and review it), they can't be bothered. And it's not because my friends are callous or hostile to my writing. I believe (I choose to believe) they just don't understand how much more important those 30 seconds would be to me than that whole day of moving. I can haul my own boxes. That's in my control. But I cannot produce the fifteen ratings and reviews that get the Amazon algorithm's attention (and I won't buy those reviews because I think that's unethical), so I desperately need that support.

Have I rated and reviewed every book I've enjoyed from every author friend of mine? Or supported every journalist or opinion columnist I've appreciated by sharing their work? No, I admit I've fallen short. But I try. And every time I do it, I'm reminded it's so much easier and faster than I thought it would be.

Consider participating in this experiment, Jiminy Cricket America. Go to Amazon or Goodreads or Barnes & Noble.com, or, if you prefer to avoid those corporate options, go to Bookshop.org or the website of your local independent bookstore, or just go to your own social media feed, and write a review of this book that starts with the words "I read it to the end, and..." After that, complete the sentence with your honest opinion, whatever that may be. "I read it to the end, and I hate this guy's guts and disagree with every word of the book." Fine. (Not fine. But fine.) Just by scrolling through the other reviews and looking for those six words, we'll all be able to see who made it this far and felt compelled to participate in supporting an author.

Of course, if you asked me directly how best to support me as an author (you haven't, but for the sake of this argument), I would encourage you to A) Buy my books, B) Read them, C) Rate and review, D) Recommend them to friends, and, if you really want to be maximally supportive, to go to my Patreon

and become a patron so you can regularly encourage me to say the things you can't say (and help me support my wife and kid and three dogs and two cats moving overseas with little more than the shirts on our backs).

And if you would rather support some other author who is staying here in the US and maybe saying something that's more aligned to what you wish you could say, please, by all means, support her. Ask her

Dear America

how, and do that.

4. Draw Your Lines Clearly and In Advance

One of my friends asked me to write a very different kind of book. Instead of an explanation of why I'm leaving, she wanted a book providing more practical guidance in case she has to uproot her family and make the same kind of move in the coming years. That book would have been very short: Don't do it the way I've done it. I had a very clear trigger that got me moving: If it came to the point that I felt the people in power would not make any effort to protect me from the people threatening to kill me, I would get out. And I gave myself a clear deadline: I would get out before those people came to power. I recommend having those clear triggers and deadlines. Here's what I didn't do: I didn't start planning to move until after my trigger was pulled. That was monumentally stupid. I was in denial. I didn't want to believe my country would get to this point, let alone the much more grim point I expect it to go to. And, not casting blame, but my wife was in even more denial than I was, and talking about it upset her. I lack the ability to think, let alone plan, without processing externally in some way. Hence this book. It's not my wife's fault I didn't prepare. I

137

could have, and should have, started writing my plans and this book long before Election Day.

Do not give yourself less than 75 days to sell your cars, sell your house, sell or donate or throw away almost everything in your house, identify a country that will accept you, learn about it's immigration system, rent an apartment, buy plane tickets, and move three humans, three dogs, and two cats around the world. That's my how-to book. Don't do this. It's stupid-fast. Oh, and while you're not doing all this in less than 75 days, also don't write a book about why you're doing it. That's insane.

Instead, Jiminy Cricket America, be like my friends who are starting to set aside funds for a move, carefully identifying potential places to move, or even making plans to do other things than move. Yes, I know people who are quietly creating networks with no digital fingerprints so they can hide immigrants from ICE or transport women across the border to get medical care. Do not wait for these things to become necessary to start planning. Spend some time now deciding what you will not stand for, and then start planning immediately for what you will do when that line is crossed. Find other people who will help you make those plans into reality should it come to that. Do that planning thoughtfully and with as little digital fingerprint as you can. Whatever it is you think you may need to do, I promise you will wish you were more ready to do it when the time comes.

5. Cut People Off, but Warn Them First

One of my family members, a white woman with a Black husband and a mixed child, posted a brave, clear, full-throated explanation of why she was cutting off Trump voters and those who didn't vote or voted third party, explaining they had made a choice that was a direct attack on her family, and she wouldn't stand for it. I love her and love everything about her post except the timing. I wish she'd made that clear weeks before the election when someone might have seen it and been taken aback, not realizing their choices would rupture relationships, and maybe would have reconsidered.

Please, be like my relative, and have the confidence and dignity and love for others necessary to cut dangerous people out of your life. Imagine the inverse. If someone is telling you that the safety and wellbeing of you and your loved ones are less important to them than a few dollars of higher prices, why would you want to be in a relationship with that person, anyway? To be polite? To be civil? You deserve better. Act like it.

And in recognizing you deserve better, recognize you have leverage. You don't need such a hateful person in your life, but they do need you, whether they can see it or not. You have the upper hand. Use it. Tell every friend and family member. Start off every first date with a clear warning. If the person says, "Well, I don't see why we need to get political," they are dismissing your values and even your life as less important than their comfort. I can just imagine someone whining that this advice will only accelerate your polarization, America. Not necessarily. If people realize their casual hatred is going to cost them, some will reconsider. But maybe it will accelerate polarization, and so what? You, Jiminy Cricket America, are under no obligation to be threatened or harmed by an ideology of hatred just so you can do your part to preserve national unity under that fascist ideology. That's not on you. Give 'em a chance to be your friends or family, and if they choose not to, let them be the strangers you will still need to live with to some extent, but upon whom you will not depend nor confide. Marginalized people know how to find this balance much better than more privileged people, keeping a safe emotional distance from those who have shown they don't care about their communities' wellbeing. It's not easy. It's painful to lose people, and it's a source of very real stress to have to treat people with a certain amount of distrust. But now us more privileged people are learning what more marginalized folx have known all along: You have to protect yourself because the hatred is cultural and systemic. So give them a chance, but, as Maya Angelou advised, when they show you who they are, believe them the first time.

There, America. Those are the t-shirts and CDs and signed books I want back from you as we end this. But I want to give you something, too.

My Last Gifts to You

America, within the timeframe of our relationship, you have given me so much. My family and friends are almost all in the U.S., every home I've lived in is within your borders, and most of my life's happy memories are with you. You gave me a free public education and even defrayed some of the cost of my (exorbitantly expensive) college and post-grad education. You gave me roads and postal service and the foundational investments that made my radio and TV and movies and Internet possible. You gave me firefighters who made me feel safe from fire, police who made me feel safe from crime (and, as a white man, feel safe from police), and sailors and soldiers who made me feel safe from foreign invasion. For all my disagreements with your excesses, I would be remiss to fail to acknowledge all you've given me.

I hope I've paid you back. I worked as a public servant, teaching your kids for 24 years. I recognize it's not always fair to measure teachers by the quality of their students, just as it's unfair to measure parents exclusively by the quality of their children. If that were an accurate measurement, I would be the best father in the world because my kids are the best, but I can't take all the credit because they have a lot of positive qualities which exceed my own and which I couldn't possibly have instilled. Similarly, my students came into my classroom, by and large, as an unusually kind, respectful, and curious group from a community which genuinely cared about them and supported them. I believe I treated them as such, and I think some of them grew into that belief in positive ways. I'm incredibly proud of the adults my former students have become, and I hope that is some repayment of my debt to you, America.

But I can read the room. You don't want me here anymore, and I don't want to watch you harm yourself, so the time has come to part ways. As I leave, I want to give you two gifts. These were given to me, but in this case I promise re-gifting is not tacky. They are more precious than any heirloom or antique one could receive and pass on. They've made an incalculable difference in my life, and if you truly accept them, I think they could be the keys to a brighter future for you. They are ideas, strings of letters forming words representing concepts of increasing complexity, less tangible than air but more important. Because what is the value of breathing to a person who cannot think? Even the simplest animal must, in some way, act on ideas like, "grow" and "feed" and "mate," and these are ideas of great beauty and power. So, please, America, accept these gifts. Chew on them, swallow them, digest them, and let them fill the marrow of your bones. They will change you.

Everyone Is Doing the Best They Can

When evaluating any other human being's behavior, start from the presupposition that they are making the best choices they know how to make in the circumstances in which they find themselves. This idea flies in the face of so much of what I was taught throughout my life. In order to teach children proper behavior, we slip into the lazy fallacy that they should make choice A rather than choice B because good people choose A and bad people choose B. This works well for parenting, temporarily. Our children, dependent upon us for approval as much as they are for food and shelter, want us to see them as "good people" and not "bad people," so if we use this formulation of "good choices" and "bad choices," they will brush their teeth and put on their shoes when we need them to. It's efficient, and it might even be appropriate, but only for so long.

Because while we are using this binary moral formulation to shape (control) their behavior, we are also exposing them to a million examples of cultural indoctrination which reinforce it. Movies where the "good people" defeat the "bad people." Religious dogma where God blesses the righteous and is wrathful towards the sinners. Social media where the cool kids get elevated and the uncool are harassed and shamed.

And at some point, when it would be developmentally appropriate to sit our kids down and challenge the notion of a moral binary, we look down the barrel of the teenage-rebellion years and decide it would just be easier if they kept on wanting to be "good people" and pleasing us rather than people making their own choices which might not align with our own.

And those kids grow up. And one day one of them is in line at the grocery store. (For the sake of ease, let's give this hypothetical young adult a name. Something you'll find non-threatening, America. A name that strikes fear into the heart of absolutely no one. Let's call him "Ben.") And Ben stands behind a person ahead of him who reeks of weed and is buying candy with food stamps, and the person has weird clothes on, and skin that's a different color, and they don't have a gender presentation Ben can clearly identify, and they have a different body type than Ben's, and when the person speaks with the cashier, they have a strange accent. And Ben simply can't help it. Ben has never been taught how to consider the possibility that everyone is doing the best they can, so Ben drops that person into one of the only two file folders in his mind. That person is now a "bad person."

And the next time Ben sees someone with similar traits and wonders where to file them, they remember the last person and decide that's where the next probably ought to go. And pretty soon, unless Ben is challenged to reconsider what he is doing, everyone with a different skin color is getting dropped in that file. Everyone with a different accent. Everyone who is a different weight. Everyone who presents their gender differently. Everyone who eats different foods or does different drugs goes into that file. (Ben's taste in drugs means those don't count as "drugs", of course. Drugs are what the "bad people" do.)

As I explain to my students, this habit of dropping ideas and impressions, including impressions of people, into categories in our minds is not evil. They should not feel ashamed about the fact that they do it. It's natural, it's human, and it's the product of evolution. Their ancient ancestors needed different files for sabretooth tigers than for harmless hippidions (those tiny horses that also lived in the same places at the same time). They needed those files because the humans who couldn't accurately assess danger, who walked towards sabretooth tigers and tiny horses alike, literally died. And thus they didn't breed, and thus they aren't my students' direct relatives. We, as humans, exist because we can make these snap judgements about our environment.

And the same adaptation that allowed us to distinguish between sabretooth tigers and tiny horses was still useful when distinguishing between people who were in our tribes and strangers who might be hostile to a tribe, so we honed the skill. Our brains are primed to distinguish between humans with a level of accuracy we don't apply to other parts of our natural world because, as we evolved, the distinction between sabretooth tigers and tiny horses became less relevant to our successful breeding than distinguishing between people who were the greater danger, so the people who lived were the ones who got really good at figuring out which file to drop people into.

This trait is so intrinsic to human existence that denying we do it is foolish. "I don't judge" is as accurate a statement as "I don't breathe." When we deny it, we're so deeply entrenched in the habit of dividing people into the "good people" and "bad people" files that we create an absurd cognitive dissonance most people don't like to explore: We think: "I don't judge because that's what bad people do." And then we get a headache and try not to think about it anymore.

America, I know not everyone (and I don't just mean children. Not every adult) is capable of deeply contemplating this insight. Some will hear "everyone is doing the best they can," and immediately get defensive because the idea challenges a conceptual framework they can't overcome. And that's okay. Ironically, their defensiveness is evidence of the truism's accuracy. They can't consider it because they are doing the best they can.

But America, as much as you are able, I hope you will try. Because the only way to escape systemic racism, sexism, xenophobia, homophobia, ableism, and other kinds of systemic oppression is to start by acknowledging their existence and own that they are not rooted in the "bad people," but in all of us.

This requires an act of what Soren Kierkegaard called "the creative imagination." When that hypothetical Ben who was indoctrinated into a binary morality sees the strange person in line at the grocery store, he has to be willing to, and capable of, considering other possibilities than the "bad people" file. He has to acknowledge he has that file, outgrow the shame he feels about the file's existence in order to find it in his mind, then reach inside it, pull his impression out, and reconsider.

Maybe the person smells like weed because they were just in a car with someone else who was hotboxing. Maybe they were smoking because they have terrible back pain and need it just to stand up straight. Maybe they suffer from terrible depression and live in a country without socialized medicine, so the best drugs for their depression aren't available to them, and weed is the closest thing they can get their hands on. Or maybe Ben could look down at his own cart and consider the possibility that the potato chips and soda and frozen bacon are his means of getting salt and sugar and caffeine and dopamine, and if someone else chooses different drugs, those aren't inherently better or worse.

Instead of assessing the person's accent as a deficiency in English, Ben could consider the possibility (which is a nigh-certainty) that the accent comes from the fact that the person learned some language other than English first. And Ben could recognize that all people start out their journey of communication first speaking to zero people, then just to a parent or sibling in a kind of code, and it's generally accepted that their communication has improved when they can communicate with more people than just Mommy. So, if being able to communicate with more people is better, it naturally follows that bilingualism is superior to monolingualism, because people who can speak to two groups of monolingual people can communicate to more than anyone in either monolingual group. For all Ben knows, the person in line might be trilingual or a polyglot who can speak seven or 10 languages. The accent might be new to Ben, but, when contrasted against a more standard English pronunciation, it's a sure sign the person is more adept at communication than a monolingual person.

Similarly, Ben might reflect on his own assumptions about weight. Why is one body type better or worse than another? Culture, not some moral failing. Maybe Ben, with his cart of potato chips and soda and bacon, who (again, completely hypothetically) is getting more exercise walking his cart around the grocery store than he's had all day, just has a very different metabolism than the other person in line. For all Ben knows, the person can lift more weight, run further, and has a heart that will keep beating twenty years after Ben's has stopped, so the erroneous notion that weight is a sign of health is really a reinforcement of cultural beauty standards and a highly profitable, powerful beauty industry selling one kind of appearance rather than several because people pay a lot more to try to look one way than they would pay to accept themselves as they are.

Which brings us to the gender presentation. Ben has been force fed ideas about gender for just as long as he's been learning about "good people" and "bad people." Girls wear dresses and make-up and nail polish and have long hair and talk out their disagreements and have lots of feelings, and boys wear pants and neckties and have short hair and call their dolls "action figures" and solve disagreements with fists and are only allowed to feel anger or amusement or nothing. Exactly zero of these things relate to human reproduction. None of them are sex characteristics. They are all gender markers, and only as defined by Ben's culture. Instead of being angry (men are allowed to be angry) or confused (men are supposed to feel angry when confused), Ben could learn to accept that this person in front of him is not a threat to his own chosen expression of his gender, and that reconsidering his own understanding of his gender is healthy. Ben might continue wearing pants if he likes them better, but he might also acknowledge that a Sikh man with hair that's six feet long is exactly as "manly" as a guy with a crew cut, and maybe Ben can even learn to admit he can be sad or confused or anxious or needy without feeling angry, and can feel elated or contemplative or deeply moved without feeling compelled to make a joke about it (maybe. Someday. Possibly). And if Ben does that, he might be able to pull out all the people he's tossed in the "bad people" file for not conforming to the gender expressions he was taught.

But what about those food stamps? Surely those are

a sign that the person is a drag on society, that they are "lazy." Whenever I've had a student teacher, I've always encouraged them to watch out for that word. It should be a screaming alarm every time they hear themselves saying it. When we look a student and say, "She's lazy," we're saying there's this one catch-all explanation for her lack of success in the classroom, and the explanation is the student's moral failing. I encourage my student teachers to take the time to consider other possibilities. Maybe she can't focus because she's hungry. Maybe she can't read the board because she needs glasses. Maybe she is struggling with some medical or psychiatric condition and needs medication. Maybe she's exhausted because she knows that when she falls asleep, her mom's new boyfriend will come into her room. In every single other possibility, she needs an adult to give her some kind of help, and when we say she's "lazy," we've chosen the one explanation that justifies refusing to give her the assistance she needs. So who is committing the moral failure? Who is being lazy?

Of course, the same rejection of that excuse should extend beyond the classroom. Very few people want to do nothing. Doing nothing is for corpses. Living people may not be able to do what we want them to do, and in that case the onus is upon us to figure out how to help them do what *they* would rather do which might be more beneficial to society as a whole. Or maybe we should reflect on what we want them to do and consider the possibility that our imposed values aren't inherently superior. Let's say one person doesn't want to have a traditional job and just wants to practice skateboard tricks all day long. Is he lazy? He gets up early, goes to the skate park, and works his ass off until the sun goes down. Compare him to the vice president at a health insurance company who maybe gets up a little later, goes to work trying to come up with ideas to make his company more profitable, and the only way to do that within our system is to conceive of new ways to deny people access to the care they need. Then he goes home before sundown to a house where a nanny has been caring for his children and a cook has made his dinner because his job is so valuable that we've allocated other people to help him with less important tasks like caring for children or preparing food. And no one calls him lazy. So maybe the person using the food stamps has fallen on hard times, but even when considering that alternate explanation, we should recognize it implies that working within the system is good, and they are merely temporarily displaced, when we could also consider the possibility that a "good person" might exist, by choice, outside the capitalist framework, and a "bad person" might exist within it.

That's challenging enough, and Ben might prefer to stop there rather than consider the characteristic he's been most deeply trained to avoid. He was pretty damned sure he didn't put the person in the "bad people" file for having a different skin color, because he was taught that judging people by the color of their skin was what "bad people" do. But if he looks in that folder, he's going to find that the othering based on every other kind of difference means the only people he was inclined to put into the "good people" who had a different skin color were the ones who didn't have the "wrong" accents or didn't wear the "wrong" clothes or didn't eat the "wrong" food or didn't listen to the "wrong" music, and who showed up to the same almost all-white church where Ben learned about what God wanted the "good people" to do, and... Holy shit! Will you look at that! All the people in Ben's "good people" folder who have a different skin color act white in every way, and there are a lot more people of color in the "bad people" folder than Ben is comfortable with. Who would have thought?

Ben will be greatly better off if he takes the time to review this filing system, because even though it started with a completely natural, human, evolutionary proclivity to identify danger mixed with a totally benign and perhaps necessary parenting technique to instill behavior that leads to household comity and functionality, the folder has grown into what Peggy McIntosh originally dubbed the "invisible knapsack" (back in 1989. This is not some radically new idea, America. You've known about this, at least to some degree, for more than thirty years). It's harmful to Ben, it's even more harmful to everyone he comes across, and it's harmful to the systems he chooses to support. Until he takes off the heavy backpack, pulls the file out, and realizes what he's doing, he will always pick systems which reduce the burden of carrying around that invisible knapsack and shift the weight, as much as possible, onto the people he's put in the "bad people" file.

You see, America, if people like this hypothetical Ben are willing to carefully examine the contents of their file folders, it could improve everything about you. Pick a problem, any problem.

Crime? Imagine a dramatic reduction in violence if men didn't feel the need to convert every bit of sadness and fear and confusion into hitting or raping women or shooting up schools.

Discrimination? Imagine if every employer was willing to stop and consider the possibility they were making decisions based on characteristics they don't even want to acknowledge they are looking for.

Education? Imagine if we all started from the assumption that every student would rather feel successful than feel unsuccessful and looked for ways to provide them the supports they need to achieve.

Healthcare? Imagine if we started from the presupposition that people are not trying to get egregious healthcare by fraudulent means but are genuinely asking for what they need because they would rather be home and healthy than sitting in a doctor's office waiting room or on hold with their insurance company while sick. If you took every dollar you spend making it profitable to deny coverage and shifted it to preventative care, you'd have millions of healthier people and a few inconvenienced billionaires who would have to make money some other way. Do you truly believe someone dying of cancer is more capable of changing their behavior because of increased copays than an executive is capable of finding a new line of work? You really think very little of your executives, America.

But wait, what about national defense? We couldn't really adopt a policy of active, intentional naiveté, could we? The libertarian ethos goes so far as to say national defense is the only purpose of a nation state because it is so rooted in this notion of "bad people" that it presupposes all other nation states are "bad people" who want to invade and conquer one another but also all government officials are "bad people" who want to oppress their own citizenry, so the only solution is to have as few as possible of the "bad people" necessary to protect a populace from the "bad people" abroad without having any extra "bad people" leading or providing services to the citizens.

But let's stop and consider this notion that government exists to protect us from invasion. America, you spend more on your military defense than the next nine highest spending countries COMBINED. If you spend only as much as the next eight, do you believe you would be invaded? The next seven? What if you just spent as much as China, Russia, and India put together? Do you think that would suddenly cause China to send one of its aircraft carriers (it has three, and you have 11) into San Francisco Bay?

Of course not. America, your investment in your military defense has very little to do with your defense anymore. You don't build ships and jets and bombs because you need them to stay safe. You build them because a Congressperson doesn't want to lose her job by closing down the bomb factory in her district. And the guy who runs that factory gives her money because he doesn't want to lose his job. And the guy working in that factory painting the American flag on those bombs doesn't want that flag to be the last thing remaining in a crater where a children's hospital used to be, but he doesn't want to lose his job. And the bomb doesn't want to do anything because it's an object, and unless it's carefully deconstructed, it has to go somewhere. So while everybody keeps their jobs, America, you give the bomb to someone you think will be a little more friendly to you than the people they drop it on. It doesn't make you safer. It's just a product of everyone doing the best they can.

And that horrible, narcissistic, murderous dictator who is commanding his army to invade the country next door? We need the bombs to save us from him, right? He's clearly a "bad person," right? No, he is also a person doing the best he can. He doesn't twist his mustache and contemplate how to build a laser beam that will slowly cut James Bond in half while he monologues about his plan for world domination. He sits up at night thinking about who he has to kill so somebody doesn't kill him, and he sends his soldiers to die in a foreign land because he thinks it's the best way to keep his people focused on something other than his failed governance. He is doing the best he knows how to do, also.

Recognizing that everyone is doing the best they can is not some Pollyanna belief that everyone is saintly and self-sacrificing. It's the acknowledgement that their behavior, even when it seems incomprehensible or maladaptive, is not malicious. People don't want to fail. They don't want to hurt. They fail and they hurt themselves and others because they don't know a better way. Everyone would choose to win if they have the option. They are just playing the only games they are allowed to play.

The guy who is buying the heroin doesn't want to be a miserable addict. He's just so deeply hopeless and is hurting so much that, when given a choice between living in that misery or feeling nothing, he chooses nothing. That's the win that's available to him in that moment. And the guy who sells him the heroin isn't evil, either. He doesn't want to be a villain. He just wants the kind of wealth and status that you, America, have told him is the only thing that will make him happy, and he doesn't know any better way to get that wealth and status than to sell heroin. And you, America, could choose to provide the heroin addict with counseling and different medication to deal with his depression, and you could choose to provide his dealer with different opportunities and a healthier idea of how to achieve happiness, but you don't know how, either. You toss them both in prison because, on some level, you have made the calculation that it's easier to call people "bad people" and lock them up than it is take care of their needs so they don't feel compelled to choose between self-destructive, maladaptive behaviors.

So start with this gift, America. Whether it's the different person in the grocery store or the different person in a prison cell or the different person sitting across the aisle in Congress, start by assuming they are doing the best they can, and then spend your energy trying to come up with ways to give them a better, healthier win.

Impact > Intent

Here is my second gift to you. This one is so important to me, I have it tattooed on my forearm so I can remind myself and others every time someone (myself included) tries to excuse harmful behavior by saying, "I didn't mean to."

Put simply, this means that regardless of a person's motivation, the outcome matters more.

I love that it's written as a mathematical formula. Imagine the words as variables. This is not saying our intentions are irrelevant. "Intent" could be pi or 50 or it could be a million. Regardless, "Impact" will be a higher number.

At first, this may seem to contradict the idea that everyone is doing the best they can, but in fact these ideas complement one another and need to be held in tension. The guy who chooses to do heroin because he's so depressed should be offered counseling and medication, but his addiction does not excuse the harm he did to his family through that addiction. The impact of his choice matters more than his motivation. The guy who was selling the heroin might only have been trying to get rich and popular, but the families that were broken, the lives his drugs upended, the people who died using the drugs he sold all matter more than his motivations. The Congressperson who made sure that bomb factory in her district stayed open might not have wanted those bombs sold to a country that would use them on another country, but the outcome is still her responsibility.

"But I didn't mean to!" Good. It's worthwhile to know a person's motivation and to understand their actions were not the product of malice. They were doing the best they could. That matters. Intent has value. But it matters less.

If we forget this, we run the risk of focusing all our attention on intent. Here's how I would always explain it to my students: I'd pick someone sitting near the front who I thought wouldn't mind the attention, and I'd stand near them. "Imagine," I'd say, "I was lecturing about some idea that got me really excited, an idea like, say, impact and intent. And I got so into it that I started swinging my arms around wildly," (I've learned to avoid the term "gesticulating" around 14 year-olds) "and I accidentally smack JJ here right in the nose. And he starts bleeding. And, horrified, I turn to all the rest of you and say, 'I didn't mean to!'

"'And then Sandra there turns to Eva and says, 'I don't know. It seemed like maybe he was trying to smack JJ,'

"And then Kyle says to Maria, 'No, Mr. Gorman isn't

that kind of person. I don't think he'd do that on purpose.'

"And then I'd get really defensive and start saying things like, 'I don't have an anti-JJ bone in my body. I have lots of friends like JJ. I even have a brother-in-law who's just like JJ. In fact, I can't even see JJ when I'm swinging my arms around."

(And while I'm saying this, I'm slowly moving around to the far side of the room.)

"And then Dawn here would say, 'I think we should believe Mr. Gorman.'

"And Brian would say, 'No we should report him to the Principal.'

"And while all of this is going on, where is all our attention focused?"

And students would shout, "At you!"

"That's right, and JJ is still bleeding. Should that be more important?"

And they got it. And they remembered it. (And they enjoyed it. We had a lot of fun in my classroom. Learning should be fun, or at least as fun as possible, even when we're learning about difficult things.)

Here's why this is so important, America. You are sliding into fascism. I may have experienced this slide a little more than some people, and I may be more sensitive to it than most because of that experience, so maybe your slide will be slower and less precipitous than I think, but the slide is real. In the midst of that slide, and especially if you ever hope to get out of it, you're going to need to hold on to these insights. The people who are choosing an ideology of hatred are not evil people. They are not the "bad people." They are people. They are scared and angry and misinformed, and when faced with a choice, they are making one that is maladaptive. It will be bad for you. You are hurting yourself. But it's the best choice they know how to make.

And that's not as important as the outcome this choice will produce. The people of Mussolini's Italy were not evil. The people of Japan under Hirohito were not evil. The people of Franco's Spain were not evil. The people of Germany under Hitler were not evil. But what they did in Ethiopia and China and Korea and Poland and in their own countries is not excused by their fear and anger and ignorance.

And you, America, have always had these tendencies as well. Japan and Germany and Spain and Italy have all reckoned with their defeats in different ways (and whether or not those efforts will save them from returning to fascism is still an open question), but you chose to tell yourself they were "bad people" and you were "good people." On the rare occasion when you are forced to look back on your worst atrocities in spite of your fervent efforts to memory-hole them entirely, you tell yourself your own horrors were committed by individuals who were un-American "bad people." No, they were done by you. Your people. A people who are not good or bad, not a nation of historical villains or a "shining light on a hill," just a group of human beings who can be misled into horrific action if you allow it.

You've already started stringing the razor wire, America. We've all seen the bodies trapped in it. The outcome has begun, and that outcome will always matter more than your excuses.

But you can choose to be better.

I just can't stay to watch you choose this.

Your Ex,

About the Author

Benjamin Gorman is an award-winning, recently retired high school English teacher, political activist, author, poet, publisher at Not a Pipe Publishing, and host of the *Writers Not Writing* podcast/YouTube show. He is now a digital nomad with his wife, bibliophile and guillotine aficionado Chrystal, their puppies, Merry and Pippin, and their pet dire wolf, Havoc. His novels are *The Sum of Our Gods*, *Corporate High School*, *The Digital Storm*, and *The Convention of Fiends* series beginning with *Don't Read This Book* and continuing in *You Were Warned*. He's also the author of two books of poetry: *When She Leaves Me* and *This Uneven Universe*.

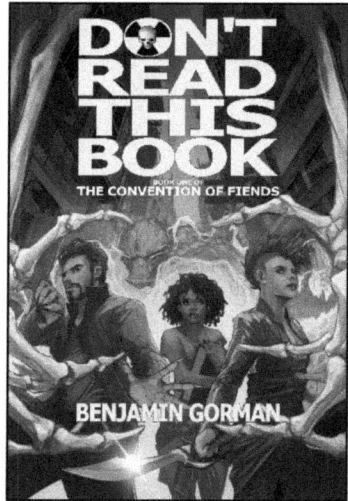

www.ingramcontent.com/pod-product-compliance
Lightning Source LLC
Chambersburg PA
CBHW070113030426
42335CB00016B/2131